ROBERT JACKSON

SUEZ

The Forgotten Invasion

SUEZ

The Forgotten Invasion

ROBERT JACKSON

Airlife
England

Copyright © 1996 Robert Jackson

First published in the UK in 1996
by Airlife Publishing Ltd

Based upon *Operation Musketeer* by Robert Jackson
and published in 1980

British Library Cataloguing in Publication Data
  A catalogue record for this book
  is available from the British Library

ISBN 1 85310 774 3

Typeset by Hewer Text Composition Services, Edinburgh
Printed in England by Biddles Ltd, Guildford and King's Lynn

Airlife Publishing Ltd
101 Longden Road, Shrewsbury SY3 9EB, England

Contents

INTRODUCTION AND ACKNOWLEDGEMENTS

Millions of words have been written about the causes and effects, the rights and wrongs, of the Anglo-French Suez operation of 1956. Most published works, however, have had a strongly political bias, and for this reason I have concentrated on the military aspects of the campaign. For any reader desiring to learn more about the political aspects of the Suez affair (which many, not without justification, might describe as a fiasco), I can do no better than recommend Keith Kyle's excellent, in-depth and intensely readable book *Suez*, the details of which will be found in the bibliography.

Keith Kyle chaired the seminar on air aspects of the Suez campaign which was held by the Royal Air Force Historical Society in 1988, and I am grateful to the management of that learned body for allowing me to draw on material contained in the relevant Proceedings. My thanks also to the staff of the Air Historical Branch, Ministry of Defence (RAF), for digging out a lot of information and photographs; in particular to Group Captain Ian Madelin, Mr Sebastian Cox, Squadron Leader Peter Singleton and Mr Alexander Zervoudakis. When last I wrote a book on Suez, in 1980, I laboured under the constraints of the Official Secrets Act; today, thankfully, it is a different story, and so, as a consequence, is the narrative I have managed to compile.

Robert Jackson
Darlington, County Durham
1996

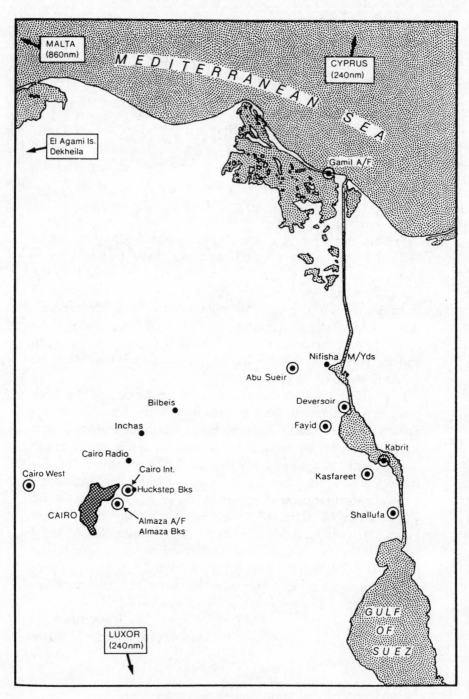

The Area of Operations

CHAPTER ONE

THE MIDDLE EAST FLASHPOINT

The Second World War had been history for a decade, and the legacy it had left was a tense and dangerous world. In every area where the war had raged there was discontent and confrontation: already, in Eastern Europe, there were signs of rebellion against the iron hand of communism; Polish workers had come into open confrontation with the authorities in the town of Poznan and elsewhere, while in Hungary, events were building into a chain reaction that would lead to explosive uprising.

The Korean War, the first major confrontation between communism and democracy, had ended in stalemate in the the summer of 1953, and had diverted attention from what was happening elsewhere in the Far East. In this unstable area, the flames of nationalism – kindled by the Japanese during World War II and since then ruthlessly exploited by the Soviet Union and Communist China – were now sweeping through the whole of South-East Asia, eroding the dwindling empires of the great pre-war colonial powers of Britain, France and the Netherlands. In Indo-China the French had taken the communist guerrillas of the Viet Minh head-on and had suffered their final humiliating defeat at Dien Bien Phu; the colonial power had relinquished its hold on the region under the terms of the 1954 Geneva armistice agreement, only to find itself embroiled in a savage conflict against nationalist rebels in Algeria.

Great Britain, for its part, had been involved in an ongoing struggle against communist terrorists in Malaya since 1948; the action there had reached its peak in 1951-2 and by 1955 the back of the communist offensive was broken, although the necessity for increased security and 'search and destroy' operations still tied down substantial numbers of troops and aircraft. Meanwhile,

1

other British forces were striving to keep Greek and Turkish factions apart in Cyprus, where the scale of atrocity against civilians was rising steadily, and in Kenya security forces had finally gained the upper hand over the dissident Mau-Mau.

April 1955 saw the departure from the political scene of Winston Churchill, under whose leadership a Conservative administration had been returned to power in October 1951. His successor was Anthony Eden, who – as Foreign Secretary during the Churchill administration – was fully aware of the problems that faced Britain and the world during the mid-1950s. He envisaged Britain's primary international role as that of mediator between the two great super-powers, the Soviet Union and the United States, both of which now had the ability to attack one another with nuclear weapons. The death of Stalin two years earlier had brought to the international scene a glimmer of hope that Russia's attitude to world affairs would now be more flexible than at any time since World War II, but there were many who doubted that Russia's internal political climate had changed at all – and her open support of terrorist groups throughout the world certainly provided no evidence to the contrary.

Elsewhere in the world, any one of several political flashpoints could conceivably lead to full-scale armed confrontation between East and West. In the Far East, the possibility of war between Nationalist and Communist China over the Chinese offshore islands – with the consequent involvement of the United States – loomed larger with every passing week. The previous months had seen a number of tense incidents in this area, including the sinking of a Nationalist frigate by Communist warships in November 1954, and in February 1955 US jet fighters shot down several Chinese MiG-15s, which had attacked them in international airspace off Formosa. The uneasy truce that followed the Korean War risked being shattered at any moment, as did the peace in Indo-China – achieved only after great personal effort at Geneva on the part of Eden himself.

Most serious of all was the situation in the Middle East, where the commercial interests of France and Britain – upheld by various treaties and the more down-to-earth presence of large numbers of troops – had come into open conflict with Arab nationalism.

2

As far as relations between Britain and Egypt were concerned, a main bone of contention was the Anglo-Egyptian Treaty of 1936, which permitted British forces to be stationed in Egypt in exchange for certain defence and security commitments. Strong nationalist sentiment in Egypt had led to a revision of the treaty in 1946, the Egyptians making it clear that the document could only be renegotiated on the basis of a complete British withdrawal from their country. After lengthy negotiations Britain reluctantly gave in to the Egyptian demands, agreeing that its forces would evacuate Cairo, Alexandria and the Nile Delta by 31 March 1947 and the rest of Egypt by 1 September 1949. There was a clause permitting British forces to return to the Canal Zone by invitation in the event of aggression 'against countries adjacent to Egypt'.

Perhaps irrationally, Britain felt herself responsible for the fate of the Middle East. It was a sentiment born of history. Twice in half a century Britain had stood in the defence of Egypt against an invader, first the Turks and more lately the Germans, and the activities of legendary adventurers such as Lawrence were still strong in the imaginations of more traditionally minded Britons. If Britain's position in the Middle East in the mid-1950s is to be fully appreciated, such sentiments must be taken in context with her commercial interests, which revolved primarily around the supply of oil. In 1955 the Middle East was the source of most of the oil used by Britain, and half that used by western Europe as a whole; and the gateway to the area's rich oilfields was the Suez Canal.

Then there was the illusion of empire, which still persisted in 1955; for Britain still stood astride much of the African continent, even though the ground under her feet was somewhat shaky. The illusion was fostered by the fact that Britain was yet the third strongest world power, both in political and military terms – although in the military sense, the idea of might was bolstered mainly by the fact that, following the lead of the the USA and USSR, although on a far smaller scale, Britain was in the process of acquiring nuclear weapons and the ability to deliver them.

Whatever the weight of criticism levelled against them, there is no doubt that the presence of large numbers of British troops in Egypt since 1882 had provided the biggest single stabilising factor in the internal affairs of the Middle East. The whole picture began to change in the years immediately after World War II, initially with the withdrawal of British forces from Cairo in 1947 and from Palestine a year later.

Continued unrest in the Middle East led to the retention of British forces in the Canal Zone base amid growing Egyptian objection. Matters came to a head when, in October 1951, the Egyptian government abrogated the treaty without warning or consultation. An extremely ugly situation developed, with the Canal Zone base compromised by insurrection and the massive withdrawal of Egyptian labour. British troops were attacked by terrorists; riots had to be put down in Ismailia; and on 25 January 1952 British forces were compelled to attack the Egyptian police barracks at Ismailia in order to pre-empt further insurrection. Reinforcements were drafted in, and contingency plans were prepared for the RAF to neutralise the Egyptian Air Force and to support British troops in an advance on Cairo. The Canal Zone was sealed off from the rest of Egypt, a move that led to an increase in Egyptian terrorist activity.

From then on, events in Egypt followed one another in rapid succession. The defeat of the Egyptian Army at the hands of Israel in 1948-49, exposing as it did the inefficiency of the army as a whole and in particular the corruption that was rife among its senior ranks, spelled the end for the rule of King Farouk. In July 1952, following a military coup – the so-called 'Colonels, revolt' in which key points around the country were seized by Egyptian forces – Farouk abdicated in favour of his infant son, who became King Ahmed Fuad II. In June 1953, however, General Neguib's military council deposed the young king and declared Egypt a republic, with Neguib himself assuming the presidency. In November 1954 Neguib himself was deposed by Lt-Col Gamal Abdel Nasser and the military council. For the time being the office of president remained vacant, presidential powers being exercised by Nasser. The latter was eventually to become president on 23 June 1956, as a result of an election at which voting was compulsory and he was the only candidate.

One immediate result of the 1952 coup was a wave of anti-British rioting and terrorist activity in Cairo and the shattering, in one blow, of British hopes for the establishment of a Middle

East defence organisation. In 1954, Britain and Egypt concluded a treaty that provided for the withdrawal of British forces from the Canal Zone by June 1956; at the same time, Britain was to retain use of the vital supply base at Ismailia in the event of any outside aggression against Turkey or any member of the Arab League – except if such aggression stemmed from Israel. By the time Eden came to power in 1955, the withdrawal of British troops from Egypt had already begun, and British civilian technicians were standing by to maintain the base facilities at Ismailia once the last soldiers had left.

As soon as the British had agreed to withdraw, the United States - who were anxious to cultivate a Middle East defence agreement including Egypt – approached Nasser with the offer of a military aid agreement, which would have enabled the Egyptians to re-equip their armed forces with modern American weapons. Nasser and his government, however, had already decided that Egypt should pursue a course of non-alignment with East and West, and the American offer was rejected.

Undeterred, the Americans went ahead with their plans to form a defence organisation in the Middle East. A mutual security and defence treaty had already been concluded between Turkey and Iraq in February 1955, and this treaty – the Baghdad Pact – was also signed by the United Kingdom, Iran and Pakistan later that year, forming the Central Treaty Organisation (CENTO). The organisation received the full backing of the United States, which – although not a full member of the Council – was a member of all major committees and bore a large share of economic and military assistance. As a direct result of US support of CENTO, relations between the United States and Egypt took a turn for the worse: since one of the member countries, Turkey, had officially recognised Israel, Nasser regarded the alliance to be treacherous to Arab interests.

It must be said, however, that dissent in the Middle East was not confined to relations between the Arabs and the European powers; internally, there was a struggle for the leadership of the Arab world between Iraq and Egypt, and enmity between Syria and Iraq as a result of the latter's desire to unify the two nations under the rule of the Iraqi royal family. This in turn led to hostility between France and Britain, for the French believed that Iraq's aspirations with regard to Syria – where French interests were still strong – were being fostered by the British government. There was growing hostility, too, between France and all the Arab nations, inspired by the conflict in Algeria. Behind the scenes there was rivalry between the United States on the one hand and Britain and France on the other, for the US State Department – anxious to achieve a commercial breakthrough in the Middle East – was beginning to cultivate relations with the Arab nationalists.

On one score, and only one, were the Arab countries united: in their bitter hatred of the tiny state of Israel, which had inflicted such a crushing defeat on her Arab neighbours during the War of Independence in 1948. In 1955, tension between Israel and the Arabs had almost reached breaking-point. Hardly a week passed without the world's newspapers reporting some serious incident along Israel's borders, such as the shooting down of Arab aircraft or exchanges of shellfire.

Egypt's intentions towards Israel were becoming increasingly militant. Despite a United Nations resolution passed in 1951, the Egyptians still prevented ships bound to and from Israel from using the Suez Canal, and there appeared to be no legal means of breaking the deadlock. The Egyptians had also occupied the island of Tiran at the entrance to the Gulf of Aqaba and set up a battery of naval guns across the straits at Ras Nasrani on the mainland, effectively denying access to the new Israeli port of Eilat.

In 1950, Britain, France and the United States had declared that they would strike up an arms balance between both Israel and Egypt, and if either side crossed the armistice lines of 1949 – held under surveillance by a small force of United Nations observers – they would 'take common counsel'. The declaration, which hinted at the possible use of force if necessary, was worthless: once the British left the Canal Zone, there would be no allied forces close enough to forestall any sudden move on the part of either the Egyptians or Israelis.

In September 1954, the Egyptians seized the Israeli vessel *Bat Galim* as she attempted to pass through the Suez Canal, and soon afterwards a number of Israelis were executed following an espionage trial in Cairo. In February 1955, by way of retaliation, the Israelis attacked the Egyptian town of Gaza, killing or wounding seventy Egyptians.

This action compelled Nasser to revise his policy and request military aid from the United States in the form of 27 million dollars' worth of arms. Because of Egypt's economic position, however, Nasser was unable to meet the State Department's demand for payment in cash, and the deal fell through. Apart from the financial considerations, the State Department also insisted that any arms supplied to Egypt should be accompanied by a supervisory group of US officers, and this Nasser refused to accept.

Nasser's immediate reaction to the Israeli attack on Gaza was to reinforce the garrison in the Gaza Strip and set up a secret commando school at Khan Yunis, where Arab volunteers – known as *fedayeen* – received intensive guerrilla warfare training. These terrorists, who were virtually suicide volunteers – the word *fedayeen* in fact means those who sacrifice themselves - were a constant thorn in the Israelis' flesh, slipping over the border to carry out their work of murder and destruction with the open acclaim of Nasser's government. In August 1955 the Israelis launched a punitive strike against Khan Yunis, killing forty Egyptians and wounding as many more; this was followed by a period of fighting along the frontier of the Gaza Strip, which lasted until the United Nations Truce Commission was able to impose an uneasy ceasefire.

Meanwhile, in May 1955, Syria had received a firm guarantee from the Soviet Union for the supply of arms from Russia. Nasser had also made approaches to the Soviet Union and Red China with a view to acquiring modern armaments, and, although China was unable to help, the Soviet government expressed its willingness to enter into negotiations. Nasser would still have preferred to purchase armaments from Britain or the United States, and at the end of May he made a final appeal to both countries, stating that if they continued in their refusal to supply military equipment he would be forced to turn to Russia. This threat appears to have been dismissed as a bluff – but negotiations between Egypt and Russia for the delivery of arms began less than four weeks later. An arms deal between Egypt and Russia's satellite, Czechoslovakia, was concluded in August 1955. It made provision for the supply to Egypt of substantial numbers of Russian-built T-34 tanks, SU-100 self-propelled guns, artillery pieces, rocket launchers, Czech-built rifles, mortars, MiG-15 jet fighters and Ilyushin Il-28 jet bombers.

With his military re-equipment programme now assured, Nasser felt justified in adopting a more militant posture with regard to Israel. In October 1955 he moved a strong concentration of troops into the demilitarised zone around Nizana, where a strategic road junction branched off towards Gaza, Rafah and Abu Agheila, the main Egyptian base in Sinai. That same month, the first batch of equipment from Czechoslovakia – including MiG-15s – reached Egypt aboard the Soviet freighter *Stalingrad*; the fighters were unloaded at Agam and taken to Almaza for assembly under the direction of a group of Czech Air Force technicians. More MiGs reached Egypt in a steady flow during the weeks that followed, assembly work being gradually taken over by Egyptian technicians who had undergone a crash training course in Czechoslovakia. The first two MiG-15 squadrons, Nos 1 and 20, formed at Almaza in December.

Israel, meanwhile, had carried out another strong counter-attack on an Egyptian frontier post in Gaza during September. Israeli anxiety about the supply of Czech arms to Egypt was growing; as yet the Israeli Intelligence Service, *Shin Bet*, did not know the full extent of the Egyptian-Czech deal, but it was clear that it presented an overpowering threat to Israel's security. At the time, Israel possessed only thirty combat aircraft – Gloster Meteor F Mk 8s – that could be considered anywhere near modern, and even these would be no match for the MiG-15. Approaches were made by the Israeli government to Canada with a view to purchasing the Canadian-built version of the North American Sabre fighter, the aircraft that had proved its worth in combat with the MiG over Korea, and negotiations got underway for the delivery of twenty-four Canadair Sabre Mk 6s. At the same time, negotiations had also begun with the French government for the supply of two principal types of combat aircraft: the Dassault Ouragan and Mystere IIC. The French agreed to supply thirty Ouragans and twenty-four Mysteres, and the first fifteen Ouragans arrived in Israel in November 1955.

In the meantime, the Canadian government had also placed

an embargo on the supply of arms to the Middle East, shattering Israeli hopes of acquiring the Sabres and leaving them totally dependent on France. In October 1955 the Israelis placed an order with France for sixty Mystere IVAs, an aircraft that could meet the MiG-15 on far more equal terms than either the IIC or the Ouragan, and the first Israeli Air Force Mystere IVA squadron, No 101, began working up in April 1956.

By then, Israel – seriously alarmed by the establishment of a unified Egyptian-Syrian military command and the stepping up of guerrilla activity along her borders – was already planning to launch a pre-emptive war against the Egyptian forces in Sinai. In November 1955 the Israeli premier, David Ben-Gurion, had instructed his Chief of Staff, Brigadier-General Moshe Dayan, to be prepared to capture the Straits of Tiran to ensure the free passage of shipping through the Gulf of Aqaba and the Red Sea. Both Dayan and Ben-Gurion advocated speedy action, but at this stage the Israeli cabinet still believed that the matter might be resolved through diplomatic negotiation and the plan was rejected.

Britain, France and the United States had also not yet abandoned hope that a policy of conciliation with Nasser might bear fruit, even though the US State Department took a somewhat jaundiced view of the Egyptian arms deal with the communist bloc. Even at the end of 1955, France embarked on an uneasy courtship with the Egyptians, promising sales of arms if Cairo's 'Voice of the Arabs' radio would cease attacks on French policy in Algeria.

These overtures were viewed with the utmost suspicion by the Israeli government, who did not discount the possibility of a secret deal between the Western powers and Nasser to the detriment of Israel. The suspicion intensified when, in December 1955, Britain and the USA offered to pay the foreign exchange costs of Nasser's projected new dam at Aswan, on the Upper Nile; the World Bank would support the project too. In return for economic aid, Nasser would back Western policy in the Middle East.

Nasser, however, was far from enthusiastic. The supply of Western equipment and know-how to enable Egyptian technicians to build the dam was one thing; the control of Egypt's economy by the West – which was what the financing of the

Aswan project by the Western powers would amount to – was another. Besides, the Russians were hinting strongly that they might be prepared to support the project, with no such strings attached.

Britain, meanwhile, was trying hard to keep the Russians out of the Middle East by pursuing the ideal of a co-ordinated defence policy within the framework of the Baghdad Pact. British hopes that Jordan would join the pact were dashed when, at the end of 1955, violent anti-British rioting – encouraged by Cairo Radio's virulent propaganda campaign – broke out in the Jordanian capital of Amman. Three Jordanian governments fell in rapid succession, and a new Prime Minister affirmed that his country would not join the Pact. The full weight of Egyptian propaganda was now turned against Iraq, the only Arab country still in the Pact.

Matters were further complicated by the French attitude to the Pact, and the French were in fact prepared to go some way towards collaborating with the Egyptians to ensure that the Pact never reached fruition. The French Foreign Minister, Christian Pineau, later stated that Nasser had promised to withdraw his support of the Algerian rebels provided that the French maintained their criticism of the Pact – a statement that was subsequently denied by Nasser himself. True or not, there was no escaping the fact that French armaments – including 155 mm howitzers and ammunition – were still being supplied to Egypt in May 1956, and in view of France's growing alliance with Israel it is difficult to understand the reason for these continuing supplies unless some tentative Franco-Egyptian agreement did exist.

In the spring of 1956 Britain – although still remaining pro-Arab in her Middle East policy – finally realised that there was no longer any hope of conciliation with Egypt. The situation was now potentially dangerous, because the last British troops were scheduled to leave Egypt in June and the question of what would happen to the Suez Canal after that was still unresolved. Then there was the Aswan Dam project, and a growing feeling that Nasser was cleverly playing the West on the end of a line while courting a better offer from the communist bloc. In May 1956, it was rumoured that the Russians had offered an interest-free loan of £50 million – by which time both Britain and the United

States were having serious doubts about Egypt's ability to repay any loan they decided to make.

In July, the British government reached a decision. In vew of the unsatisfactory political situation in the Middle East, and the growing conviction that any financial commitment to Egypt would prove too onerous, Britain would withdraw from the Aswan project. For Nasser, the news that the West had irrevocably lost interest in the Aswan project came as no surprise; he had been expecting such a decision for some time. What he had not been expecting was a complete reversal of the Soviet Union's attitude. On 22 July – only days after Britain's decision to withdraw from the scheme – Dmitri Shepilov, the Russian Foreign Minister, suddenly denied publicly that the Soviet Union had offered to finance the building of the dam. For the Egyptians, that left only one other possible source of revenue: the Suez Canal.

On the evening of 26 July 1956, in the course of a three-hour speech to a vast crowd assembled in Alexandria's Liberation Square, Nasser proclaimed the Egyptian government's decision to nationalise the Suez Canal Company, the international agency which, under a teaty in existence since 1888, had been authorised to operate the Canal on behalf of all users. He seized control of the Company's Egyptian offices, ordered all obligations, rights and funds to be transferred to the Egyptian State, declared martial law in the Canal Zone, and ordered all employees of the Company – including foreigners – to remain at their posts. It was an act of piracy on an international scale.

The assembled crowds screamed their approval. They streamed through the streets, shouting anti-British slogans. In the harbour, the crew of the British cruiser HMS *Jamaica* closed to action stations and prepared to use force if the demonstration became more violent. Nasser returned to Cairo that night with the knowledge that there could be no turning back now. What he could not know was that he had set the stage for one of the biggest political and military fiascos in history.

CHAPTER TWO

REACTIONS AND INITIAL DEPLOYMENTS

Long before Nasser's abrupt nationalisation of the Suez Canal Company, the British Prime Minister, Anthony Eden, had been forming an impression that, as he put it, 'Nasser was determined to wreck us.' Events in Jordan, where extreme nationalism was being stimulated by Egypt, Syria and Saudi Arabia, together with the virulent anti-West campaign by Cairo Radio, served to underpin this impression. Furthermore, intelligence reports from the Middle East agencies of MI6 indicated that Nasser was a wholly-dominated agent of the Soviet Union – which belief, as a matter of interest, was not shared by America's Central Intelligence Agency.

The first reaction to Nasser's proclamation, in both London and Paris, was one of expected militancy. For the British, it was mainly a matter of prestige; for the French, a matter of regarding the Suez Canal as their own undertaking. However, at a meeting of British Ministers and Service Chiefs held in the evening of 26 July it was decided that it was not possible to make any form of instant retaliation. On the following day the Cabinet met, and an extract from the Minutes shows the prevalent feeling:

> The Cabinet agreed that we should be on weak ground basing our resistance on the narrow ground that Colonel Nasser had acted illegally. The Suez Canal Company was registered as an Egyptian company under Egyptian law and Colonel Nasser had indicated that he intended to compensate its shareholders at ruling market prices. From a narrow legal point of view his action amounted to no more than a decision to buy out the shareholders. Our case must be presented on wider international grounds. Our argument must be that the Canal was an important international asset and

facility, and that Egypt could not be allowed to exploit it for a purely internal purpose. The Egyptians had not the technical ability to manage it effectively.

The last sentence was condescending, and its sentiment was wrong. By mid-September 1956, Egyptian personnel were controlling the movement of shipping through the Canal very efficiently, all foreign staff other than Greeks having been sacked.

The Cabinet Minutes of 27 July continued: 'It was evident that the Egyptians would not yield to economic pressures alone. They must be subjected to political pressure and, in the last resort, the political pressure must be backed by the threat, and if need be, the use of force.'

The decision on the use of force as a last resort was unanimous, although some Cabinet members – like the Minister of Defence, Walter Monckton, for example – were to have second thoughts in the weeks to come. As it was, a crisis management group called the Egypt Committee was quickly set up, comprising the Chiefs of Staff and a fairly small group of Ministers. The minutes of its first meeting, on 30 July, leave no doubt about its agreed objectives:

> While our ultimate purpose was to place the Canal under international control, our immediate purpose was to bring about the downfall of the present Egyptian Government. This might, perhaps, be achieved by a less elaborate operation than those required to secure physical possession of the Canal itself.

The French Government was of like mind. On that same day, Colonel Prieur of the French Army Staff arrived in London and indicated that France was prepared to commit two divisions to any action against Egypt; the French were in favour of launching such an operation at the earliest possible date.

In fact, the initial instruction to the Chiefs of Staff to prepare a military plan for operations against Egypt had been issued on 29 July, and an outline plan was drawn up within 48 hours. On 2 August, the British public received the first indication that military operations against Egypt might be set in motion when the Prime Minister informed the House of Commons that 'Her Majesty's Government have thought it necessary to take certain precautionary measures of a military nature. These measures include the movement from this country of certain Army, Navy and Air Force units'.

Also on 2 August, a Royal Proclamation was issued, calling up a number of reservists – mainly specialists and technicians from Sections 1 and 2 of the Army Emergency Reserve – and retaining all regular troops due for discharge. At the same time, it was announced that the return of National Servicemen from overseas might be delayed by 'extensive troop movements and precautionary measures in the Mediterranean area.'

The first of the 'precautionary measures' involved the assembly of units of the French Fleet at Toulon and the hurried despatch of three British aircraft carriers – HMS *Bulwark*, HMS *Theseus* and HMS *Ocean* – to join HMS *Eagle* in the Mediterranean. RAF Transport Command's routine worldwide services were also cancelled, and units ordered to stand by for a major airlift operation. Units of Bomber Command were also alerted in readiness for a rapid deployment overseas, as were a battalion of the Life Guards and a battalion of the Grenadier Guards, stationed at Windsor.

It was not as simple as it sounded, for as military planning went ahead the problems facing Britain and France, in terms of both equipment and logistics, became all too apparent. While it was true that units of both the British and French Mediterranean Fleets could be on station off the coast of Egypt within a matter of days, it was also true that the carrier-borne aircraft, which would have to play a key part in any air attack programme on Egyptian targets, were sadly outclassed by Nasser's Soviet-built combat aircraft. The complement of the two French carriers in the area – the *Lafayette* and *Arromanches* – consisted entirely of piston-engined Corsairs and Avengers; the equipment of HMS *Eagle*, the only British carrier in the Mediterranean at the time of Nasser's speech, comprised more modern Sea Venom and Sea Hawk jets, but even these would be no match for the MiG-15. Neither would the RAF's Venom fighter-bombers, with which squadrons in the Middle East were equipped at the time. The only RAF fighter that could meet the MiG on advantageous

14

terms was the Hawker Hunter, and the few squadrons so far equipped with the type were based in the United Kingdom. The French Air Force possessed several squadrons of Mystere IVs and F-84 Thunderstreaks, but these were all based in either France or Germany and it would take at least two weeks to transfer some of them and their supporting equipment to the Mediterranean. In Algeria, the most modern French combat aircraft was the Mistral, the licence-built version of the de Havilland Vampire.

It was also clear that Cyprus, established as the main RAF base in the eastern Mediterranean after the final withdrawal from the Canal Zone in May 1956, was the key to any air operations against Egypt. At the end of July the main airfield, Akrotiri, housed three front-line units: No 6 Squadron with Venoms, No 13 (PR) Squadron, which was in the process of exchanging its Meteor PR 10s for Canberra PR 7s, and No 208 Squadron, armed with Meteor FR 9s. The station was also the home of No 103 Maintenance Unit, the RAF Hospital and No 3 Wing of the RAF Regiment, with two light anti-aircraft squadrons.

RAF Nicosia, the only other usable airfield on the island, housed four squadrons: No 73 (Venoms), 70 (Hastings), and 84 and 114 (Valettas). In addition the airfield was home to No 113 MU and Nos 2 and 34 RAF Regiment squadrons. It was badly overcrowded.

The first RAF reinforcement to Cyprus departed the UK on 3 August, and comprised four PR Canberras of No 58 Squadron from Wyton, in Huntingdonshire. A fifth Canberra followed on the 26th. At Tangmere, personnel of Nos 1 and 34 Squadrons, with barely a week's notice, made Herculean efforts to get their Hawker Hunter Mk V aircraft ready for deployment to Akrotiri; the Hunters arrived there on 8 August and were fully operational within 36 hours, providing the island with a modern air defence element. Eight Meteor NF 13 night fighters were also deployed to Akrotiri from Luqa, Malta, shortly afterwards, exchanging bases with the Meteor FR 9s of 208 Squadron. Apart from the fact that Akrotiri was now badly overcrowded, the Meteor FR 9 did not have sufficient range to be of use in operations over Egypt.

As far as in-theatre ground forces were concerned – that is to say those in place on Cyprus – many were, in 1956, committed to operations on the island against the EOKA terrorists; the British forces included two battalions of the 16th Parachute Brigade, two battalions of the Royal Marine Commando Brigade, and eight infantry battalions.

The Cyprus operations had seriously interfered with the routine training of both paratroops and Marines. It was a year since the latter had been able to take part in an amphibious assault exercise, and almost as long since the paratroops had carried out an airdrop. The only amphibious warfare squadron in the area was based on Malta. This consisted of two tank landing ships (LSTs), each of which was able to carry eight assault landing craft and two tank landing craft – completely inadequate for the size of operation envisaged. Some assault equipment left over from the Normandy landings twelve years earlier was still stored in the UK, but most of it had been sold abroad or auctioned for scrap. Some of the former British landing craft were, in fact, still in service with the French Navy.

Apart from the forces available in Cyprus, the only other units that were in a position to take part in an immediate assault on Egypt were the French 10th Parachute Division and the 7th Mobile Mechanised Division, both of them based in Algeria. The British 10th Armoured Division was in Libya and the 10th Hussars in Jordan, but since they were both based in Arab countries their use against Egypt would almost certainly lead to dangerous repercussions.

At this time, early in August, the British and French governments had not yet committed themselves to active operations against Egypt. There were still hopes that some form of negotiation might still be successful, and Eden's overwhelming concern was to secure American support. To this end urgent talks were held between the British government on the one hand and the American Secretary of State, John Foster Dulles, on the other. The Americans, anxious to play for time, advocated further attempts at conciliation and the arranging of a top-level conference aimed at the internationalisation of the Canal. If Nasser rejected the conclusions of such a conference, there might then be a case for joint military action.

Despite all the obvious uncertainty, preparations for the invasion of Egypt went ahead, but the British Chiefs of Staff came out firmly against the immediate use of force. Although it was theoretically possible for paratroops to go in immediately and capture key points on the Canal, there was no logistics organisation to support them subsequently and a hasty decision of this kind was almost certainly bound to lead to disaster.

On 7 August, joint talks began in London between the British and French military staffs. The overall aim was to form an integrated Anglo-French command system under a British commander; he would have a French deputy, and each service involved would follow a parallel system. Cyprus would be the operational base.

On 11 August, General Sir Charles Keightley GCB GBE DSO – Commander-in-Chief British Land Forces Middle East – was appointed to be Supreme Allied Commander, with Vice-Admiral d'Escadre Pierre Barjot, Commander-in-Chief French Mediterranean Fleet, as his deputy. Command of the land forces was vested in Lieutenant-General Sir Hugh Stockwell, commander of the British 1st Corps in Germany; his deputy was General Andre Beaufre, who had been recalled from commanding the 2nd Mechanised Infantry Division in Algeria.

The allied naval forces were to be commanded by Vice-Admiral Maxwell Richmond, with Contre-Admiral Lancelot as his deputy. Richmond was later replaced by Vice-Admiral Robin Durnford-Slater. Responsibility for the air element rested with Air Marshal Denis Barnett, whose deputy was Brigadier-General Raymond Brohon.

To undertake an operation of the scope envisaged, it was decided initially to commit 80,000 troops: 50,000 British and 30,000 French. At this stage, no firm decision had been taken to spearhead an assault with airborne forces; even if such a decision was taken, the number of paratroops employed would be strictly limited by the relatively small numbers of available British and French transport aircraft, and it was clear that the greater part of the invasion force would have to be transported by sea. Hundreds of vessels of all types, ranging from troopships and tankers to landing craft, would be needed, as well as over a hundred warships to escort them and provide firepower during the landings. The problems confronting the assembly of such an armada, and the loading of men, stores and equipment, were stupendous. Cyprus's principal harbour of Famagusta was completely inadequate in terms of both size and quay facilities for a major provisioning operation; it was so shallow that any vessel of over 5,000 tons would be denied access, and would have to stand a mile offshore. The port of Limassol was even worse, with no wharf facilities at all. All stores here would have to be loaded by lighter.

Because of these considerations, the Allied planners turned their thoughts towards the possibility of a landward thrust into Egypt by the 10th Armoured Division in Libya, following the route taken by Rommel's Afrika Korps in World War II. This, however, was soon discounted, for such a move would depend on securing the approval of the Libyan government, and since it involved the use of force against another Arab state it was unlikely that approval would be forthcoming.

The only alternative was to assemble the invasion force on Malta – nearly 1,000 miles and a week's sailing time away from Egypt, which meant that any element of surprise would be lost. It was therefore generally agreed that Malta would be the main assembly base, despite all the obvious disadvantages.

It was still not clear what the invasion force was going to do once it reached Egypt. The overall aim was to occupy the Canal Zone, but this basic strategy was already clouded by political thoughts of overthrowing Nasser and his government, which in turn influenced the choice of objectives. If the main object was to seize the Canal Zone for the purpose of safeguarding Allied interests, the capture of key points along the Canal might be sufficient; on the other hand, the deposing of the Egyptian government would mean a drive on Cairo, with the destruction of the Egyptian armed forces and the occupation of the entire country.

In the latter case, with Cairo as the main objective, the most suitable Egyptian port for an Allied landing would be Alexandria, which was well enough equipped to handle the largest sea traffic. An initial bridgehead here could be rapidly reinforced, and a two-pronged thrust towards Cairo and the Canal could soon be initiated. The main disadvantages in the choice of Alexandria lay in the fact that any drive towards the Canal would have to cross the

Nile Delta, which was densely populated and well suited to defensive action.

From the geographical point of view, Port Said was a much more favourable position, lying at the northern end of the Canal. A rapid drive from here through to Suez would not only place the whole of the Canal in Allied hands, but would also split the Egyptian Army in two. The facilities in Port Said, however, were far from adequate for coping with large-scale loading and unloading operations, and because of its position on a peninsula the exit routes from it would be vulnerable to enemy attack. From Port Said, the roads and railway followed a narrow strip of land adjacent to the Canal for twenty-five miles as far as El Kantara, crossing the two principal bridges on the outskirts of the port. The capture of these bridges was of paramount importance to a fast breakout from the port; equally as vital was a fast drive along the 25-mile causeway, where the advance could easily become bogged down in the face of enemy resistance.

During the first two weeks of August, there was a great deal of travelling to and fro on the part of the Allied commanders and their staffs between London, Cyprus, Toulon, Paris, Malta, Algiers and Libya. Apart from the problem of having key personnel dispersed over a wide area, other complications arose; not the least of them was the language barrier. Only a handful of French and British personnel had more than a schoolboy knowledge of each others' language; this could be a serious shortcoming in action, when British signallers would be required to call on French air and naval support and vice versa. In the end, the Allies arrived at a solution of sorts by exchanging signallers who were reasonably proficient in both languages.

By 15 August the first outline of the plan had begun to take shape. The deadline for its completion was fixed for the middle of September, when everything had to be ready for the assault. The original codename for the operation was *Hamilcar* – a reference to Hamilcar Barca, the Carthaginian general who had a long history of succesful campaigns. Units were ordered to paint the initial letter of the name on their vehicles for identification purposes – and even here the difference in language reared its head, for the

French spelling of the name was Amilcar. Within a matter of days the codename had been changed to *Musketeer*, a name that was eminently acceptable to both French and English.

CHAPTER THREE

THE MUSKETEER PLAN

While initial planning went ahead, the Egypt Committee decided that a meeting of the twenty-two maritime powers with interests in the Canal would have to be held. There was an underlying reason behind this move, as stated in the Minutes:

> The purpose of the maritime conference was to be limited to the approval of a declaration of policy which had formed the basis of a note to the Egyptian Government, which we would be prepared, if necessary, to despatch on our own responsibility, and which would be a virtual ultimatum. If Colonel Nasser refused to accept it, military operations would then proceed.

The conference was held at Lansdowne House in London on 16 August, and of all the nations invited only Egypt and Greece failed to turn up, the latter because of the EOKA insurrection in Cyprus, which was then at its height. Eighteen of those which did attend supported a United States plan for the Suez Canal to be subject to control by an international board with Egypt fully represented on it and guaranteed a reasonable financial return. In the event, despite lengthy diplomatic negotiations headed by the Australian Prime Minister, Sir Robert Menzies, this plan came to nothing.

While diplomatic activity continued, the Egypt Committee raised the question of whether: 'the aim could be achieved by unseating the present Egyptian Government by bombing alone. If so, the operation could start relatively quickly. The bomber force could be in position in a fortnight and could start full bombing operations in a further week.'

It was an extraordinary point of view, given all the experience

21

to the contrary that had emerged from World War II and Korea. Moreover, there was another problem: there were not sufficient stockpiles of bombs on Malta, from where attacks would have to be launched, and it would take the whole of August and September for the necessary stockpiles to be built up, the Main Force Canberra squadrons of RAF Bomber Command being used to ferry 1,000 lb bombs from the UK to Malta. In any case, the idea of ousting the Egyptian Government by bombing alone was rejected on the grounds that it would not achieve the full objective of the operation.

As far as the emerging operational plan was concerned, it was very similar in broad outline to the invasion tactics developed by the Allies in the Mediterranean Theatre during World War II. The first task was to achieve total air superiority; once this had been accomplished, the seaborne invasion was to be preceded by an airborne assault. With a firm beachhead secured, troops and material would then be poured ashore under covering fire from the Allied fleet.

The plan in itself, however, led to differences of opinion in the British and French High Commands. The French regarded it as too ponderous: they were firmly in favour of speedy action, with the actual landing preceded by a very short and very intense period of air attack. The British, on the other hand, envisaged up to six days of air attacks – the length of time, in fact, that the convoys from Malta would be at sea – and they were against the idea of the invasion fleet sailing until all hope of a political compromise had vanished.

The French viewpoint was summed up by General Beaufre, who later wrote[1]:

> First, what was the object of the operation? I had no directive on this subject but it was clear that, from the French point of view, the target was Nasser; his was the revolution which was setting alight and unifying the Arab world. We must therefore defeat the Egyptian Army and go to Cairo. Any more limited operation would leave the dictator's government in being and allow him to rouse world opinion through the radio. Moreover if we did not, directly or indirectly, take over the reins of government in Egypt, a guerrilla resistance movement similar to that which

had just driven the British from the Canal Zone would soon make its appearance. It was therefore essential that we should have available the forces necessary for a decisive operation, with the proviso that its scope could be limited if the political object had been achieved before it was fully underway.

The original plan called for the capture of Alexandria by means of an airborne drop south-west of the town, followed by a seaborne assault, and then a drive on Cairo. The British forces were to capture the port, while French air- and seaborne forces secured the western and south-western exits from the town. One week would be allowed for the concentration of Allied forces in the beachhead before the advance on Cairo, and the battle for the Egyptian capital would be fought between D+6 and D+14. The subsequent thrust eastwards to Suez would be assured either by the capture of the Cairo bridges across the Nile, or by a French paratroop operation on the Nile Delta Barrage.

It was accepted by both French and British that the Alexandria operation would be risky and possibly attended by heavy losses, particularly in its early stages. Submerged reefs made the approaches to both the main and secondary beaches at Alexandria dangerous, and the beaches themselves – according to the latest intelligence reports – were being heavily mined. There was also the possibility that the paratroop dropping zone, some distance away to the south of Lake Mariut, might be cut off by Egyptian armour before Allied support could arrive. Air Chief Marshal Sir Denis Smallwood, who was then Group Captain (Plans) Air Task Force, recalls[2]:

> We got to the first floor underground (in the Air Ministry) and I was ushered into what turned out to be a kind of conference room full of people and a very strong smell of Gauloise cigarettes, which I thought was odd. At the end was a man with a pointer, pointing at a map of Egypt, and his opening words which I locked on to were 'And so, gentlemen, it's settled then. It'll be a combined assault on Alexandria, with a break-out on the road to Cairo. We shall then swing east across the Delta and occupy the whole of the Canal.' I felt a slight feeling of nausea. Had there been a bar down there (which there wasn't – another oversight in the planning) I would immediately have taken a double brandy.

It was not just the risks involved in implementing the Alexandria plan that gave cause for concern. In the first week or two of August Britain was extremely anxious over France's notoriously poor security, to the extent that initially the British were not prepared to reveal the full nature of their planning to their Allies until the latter had conformed to the British system of security. Guy Mollet, the French Premier, agreed to this and Patrick Dean, Chairman of the Joint Intelligence Committee, was sent to Paris to brief the French on the methods of security that were to prevail during the operation. His aim was that only two French politicians, the Prime Minister and the Minister of Defence, should be privy to all the planning secrets. Following this, a system of security was established, covering especially the conveyance of documents between London and Paris, which worked very well.

Despite any misgivings the Alexandria plan went ahead, and by 18 August the finishing touches were being put to it. The landings were to take place on 15 September – the earliest possible date envisaged, with the go or no-go decision to be taken on 30 August – preceded by two days of air strikes, and two clear weeks had to be allowed for the assembly of the invasion force.

On 22 August the military programme was postponed by four days. The reasoning was that if the initial timetable were to be adhered to, violations of Egyptian airspace for necessary photo-reconnaissance would have to be authorised at once, and Eden thought that this was not a good idea while conference was still in progress.

The final seal of approval was to be set on the Alexandria plan at a meeting of the Joint Chiefs of Staff in London on 25 August, presided over by General Keightley. The meeting had hardly begun when, quite out of the blue, the French – through Admiral Barjot and General Gazin – proposed an alternative to the Alexandria operation in the form of a landing at Port Said. Keightley and Stockwell, once they had got over their initial surprise, agreed to study the new plan – although they did not seriously believe that the Allies could embark on an entirely new concept at this stage of the proceedings.

Preparations for the Alexandria landing continued, and a

timetable was drawn up. In Malta and Algeria, British and French troops earmarked for the operation began an intensive phase of training, culminating in a joint Anglo-French amphibious assault exercise on Malta on 5 September. Both British and French were experiencing serious logistics problems, with the result that the operation was further postponed. The landings would now take place on the 25th.

Behind the scenes, however, political forces were at work that, within days, would turn the carefully laid plans upside down. Egypt had now rejected every Allied compromise proposal, which meant that Anthony Eden and the French Premier, Guy Mollet, were now faced with the decision to order the invasion to go ahead. They met on 10 September in London, and the first decision they made was that the objective should be changed from Alexandria to Port Said. Once the Canal Zone was occupied, it was generally agreed that there would be an Allied drive westwards on Cairo.

The reasons for the change were varied and complex. First of all, political opinion in the United Kingdom was moving firmly against an attack on Cairo, and as far as Mollet and his ministers were concerned the Alexandria plan was to cumbersome. They advocated a swifter scheme, making greater use of airborne forces to seize the Canal Zone in a few hours. Then there was the American attitude to be considered; in a series of lengthy telegrams to the British and French Prime Ministers, Dulles advocated a new scheme known as the Suez Canal Users' Association, a projected international organisation that would deal with all problems of passage through the Canal. Even if Nasser refused to accept the proposal, Eden thought that Britain, France and the USA might bring it off together. However, as he remarked to the Home Secretary, he personally thought it a 'cock-eyed idea, but if it brings the Americans in, I can go along'.

A second London Conference was convened on 19 September to establish formally the Suez Canal Users' Association, even though the scheme had already been denounced by Nasser. It was to comprise the 18 nations who had originally voted for it, together with any other Canal users who wished to join. Its failure was almost a foregone conclusion, as a resolution of six principles for a negotiated settlement tabled before the UN Security Council was rejected by Egypt and vetoed by the Soviet Union. If Anthony Eden had wished for a *casus belli*, he had one now.

Logistics factors played an important part in influencing the switch from Alexandria to Port Said, and it is useful at this point to look at the size of the forces allocated to the operation. On the British side, there were 45,000 men, 12,000 vehicles, 300 aircraft and 100 warships; on the French side, 34,000 men, 9,000 vehicles, 200 aircraft and 30 warships. The airborne assault would be undertaken by the British 16th Independent Parachute Brigade and General Massu's 10th Airborne Division, while the nucleus of the seaborne assault would consist of the British 3rd Commando Brigade, supported by one regiment – 48 Centurion tanks – of the 10th Armoured Division. Behind them would come the British 3rd Infantry Division, sailing from the United Kingdom, and the French 7th *Division Mecanique Rapide* from Algeria. The whole was comparable to the Allied force assembled for the assault on Anzio in 1944.

As planning for the original Alexandria operation progressed during August and early September, it began to be obvious that – because of the critical shortage of landing craft and seaborne transport of all types, as well as the lack of base facilities – a force of this magnitude would prove too unwieldy to meet the demands of a limited time schedule such as that envisaged in the Alexandria landings. It was doubtful whether sufficient stores, equipment and reinforcements could be put ashore in the six-day period set aside before the planned drive on Cairo, and yet any holdup in the timetable might prove fatal in an operation where speed was of the essence.

The seizure of Port Said and limited objectives in the Canal Zone – which could conceivably be held for a lengthy period by the paratroops and Marines with full Allied air superiority, enabling the main seaborne forces to disembark more or less at leisure – therefore seemed to present a far more acceptable solution.

Nevertheless, the logistics problems were still formidable, and the difficulties were not eased by the fact that the logistics arrangements had to be changed with every alteration to the main plan. Apart from the necessity to build up vast depots and stores of fuel on Malta and Cyprus, the lack of airfield facilities on the latter island – without which the airborne assault could not take place – posed a severe headache. In August 1956 only one of the three Cyprus airfields that could accept transport aircraft – the international civil airport of Nicosia – was operational, and even then extensive construction work severely limited the space available for parking large numbers of aircraft. The RAF base at Akrotiri was being expanded, with a great deal of new construction underway, and was one of EOKA's principal targets. It would be the middle of October before both fields were fully operational, and both were allocated for RAF use during the emergency. The French were assigned to Tymbou, five miles from Nicosia on the main road to Famagusta; this had been used only as an emergency landing ground, and a crash development programme was begun in August to make it fit for use by the French transport aircraft. In the light of these known deficiencies, the new date fixed for the Port Said landing – 1 October – appears totally unrealistic.

To meet the schedule, the first ships would have to leave England on 21 September at the latest – and it was now the 12th. There was no time for anything like a complete revision of the loading plans; all that could be done was to re-assign the forces destined for Alexandria to objectives of more or less similar importance in Port Said. The plan itself was therefore merely an adaptation of the original idea, and was known as *Musketeer Revise*.

Port Said was now the British objective, while the French were to land further east at Port Fuad. Both forces would then drive southwards, with the British on the west bank of the Canal and the French on the east. On reaching El Kantara the British were to push westwards to Abu Sueir, while the French were to cross over to the west bank of the Canal to take Ismailia and Suez. The British and French were then to join forces in a two-pronged drive on Cairo from Abu Sueir and Suez.

If everything went according to plan, the French estimated that the Canal Zone could be occupied in four days; the more conservative British estimate was between a week and ten days. The codeword that would launch the operation was to be *Toledo*. Although details of the plan were subjected to many variations, the basic structure remained the same as preparations went ahead. First of all, an intensive series of air strikes would eliminate the Egyptian Air Force, after which the weight of Allied air power would be turned on the Egyptian coastal defences. These would be subjected to a further bombardment by naval guns; this would last for an hour and cover the assault force, which was scheduled to hit the Port Said beaches thirty-five minutes after sunrise. Thirty minutes after the first landing, the paratroops would be dropped on their objectives. While the Egyptian garrison was being overwhelmed, minesweepers would open up a passage into the harbour, and it was hoped to get tanks ashore within three hours. By this time the seaborne force should have joined up with the paratroops, opening the way for the armour to proceed down the Canal road towards Suez.

The plan in itself – although feasible enough on paper – laid bare the serious misgivings that had been voiced for some time by senior commanders about the very severe shortcomings in Britain's postwar defence policy. All three services, their resources whittled away steadily since the end of World War II, now found themselves faced with a serious manpower crisis. Men were desperately needed to bring the regular units up to strength, and other units – such as those concerned with the operation of railways, port and dock facilities, which were not included in the peacetime order of battle – had to be mobilised from the Army Emergency Reserve. Men who were called up found themselves kicking their heels in depots and training regiments with little or no sense of urgency, which did nothing to improve their morale. Some reservists – and this was particularly true of the paratroops – were well trained and slipped back into active military life easily; others had been out of touch for so long that they were useless. Nevertheless, despite being dragged away from their jobs and homes at such short notice and for an indefinite period, most of the reservists settled down stoically enough to see the emergency through.

Of the formation earmarked to carry out the initial assault, most of the 3rd Commando Brigade and two battalions of the 16th Parachute Brigade Group were in Cyprus, engaged in Operation Pool Bull – the search for the terrorist Lenas gang, which was reported to be in the Troodos Mountains. On 10 August the Commandos were relieved in their sector by units of the Gordon Highlanders, and four days later No 45 Commando embarked in HMS *Theseus* at Famagusta and sailed for Malta, where a period of intensive training lay ahead. Much emphasis lay on co-operation with tanks, as the plan called for the landing of an armoured regiment with the assault force. Since it was not thought likely that the Libya-based 10th Armoured Division could be used, it was decided early in August to raise a new armoured brigade as part of the 3rd Infantry Division in the United Kingdom, and one of its units – the 6th Royal Tank Regiment – was placed on the order of battle for invasion. One of No 45 Commando's officers later described the training in Malta[3]:

> We had barely time to get re-accustomed to the idiosyncrasies of Ghain Tuffieha Camp before we found ourselves in the midst of an intensive training programme. Three full-scale amphibious exercises in quick succession punctuated troop training, and two "set piece" exercises with live enemy run by the unit for each rifle troop in turn. A troop of LVsT (Landing Vehicles Tracked, or Buffaloes) were living with the unit at this time and much training was done with them, although we never worked with them operationally. "A" Squadron, 6th Royal Tank Regiment, drove up from Marsa at dead of night and spent a week on Mayesa field firing range, during which time each troop did an exercise with two troops of tanks, which was of great value. It was felt by the infantry, however, that realism had over-stepped the mark when the umpires made them wear respirators for half an hour during an uphill assault; even the fittest Marine formed the opinion that a death by gassing would be preferable to drowning in his own perspiration.'

In the case of other units, training was very much an improvised business. Troops of 81 Port Regiment, for example, who were flown to Cyprus at the end of August and who would have to supervise the unloading of stores and equipment during the actual operation, spent weeks working with the dockers at Famagusta, helping to unload merchant cargoes. As well as assisting in the build-up of the Cyprus depots, this activity had an immense training value.

Two armoured regiments – the 1st and 6th Royal Tanks – were included in the original order of battle, and the state of readiness of both units left much to be desired. One of the 1st Royal Tanks' squadrons had no armoured vehicles at all, its personnel working as mechanics with the Territorial Army; another squadron was being used for training at the School of Infantry, and the third was on garrison duty at Tidworth. The 6th Royal Tanks had recently completed a tour in Germany, and many personnel were still there; the remainder were scattered throughout the United Kingdom, working with the Territorials.

The reorganisation of both regiments was chaotic. Much of the equipment issued to them from depots up and down the country was outmoded and totally inadequate; some of it dated back to 1940. Many of the vehicles also lacked essential items of equipment such as wireless aerials and ammunition racks.

Transporting the armoured regiments to their UK embarkation ports proved a nightmare for everyone involved. The weight of the Centurion tanks made movement by rail out of the question, which meant that the journey from Tidworth to Southampton and Portland had to be made on road transporters. Since the Army had only a handful of these vehicles, they had to call on the services of the civilian firm of Pickfords, who used heavy transporters to move large components for industry. Pickfords' crews, however, were tied to union working hours, which meant that they took a week to do a trip that could have been made by Army crews in half the time. The result was that the move took four weeks, two of which might otherwise have been spent in valuable training.

The 6th Royal Tanks, with 47 Centurions, finally sailed for Malta on 4 September. Because of all the transportation delays it was to be nearly two months before the 1st Tanks followed it. To complicate matters even further, out of the 32 tank landing ships available on paper to transport the regiments to the Mediterranean, only two were actually in service; the rest were in storage and had to be made seaworthy when their cocoons were removed. Only twelve more could be made ready in time.

There was also a critical shortage of vessels suitable for

trooping. The first ships to be pressed into service in this role were the aircraft carriers *Ocean* and *Theseus*, which sailed for the Mediterranean at the end of July. Both vessels had been serving for some time as training ships and were no longer equipped to operate aircraft. A third carrier in British home waters, HMS *Bulwark*, had also been used for training, with her operational squadrons at shore bases. After embarking three squadrons of Sea Hawk Mk 6s she also sailed for the Mediterranean, arriving at Gibraltar on 9 August. Three days later she joined HMS *Eagle* off Malta and began an intensive period of flying training, her crews carrying out close-support operations in conjunction with No 45 Commando, air-to-air firing, practise shipping strikes on the frigate HMS *Ulysses* and the French carrier *Arromanches*, and low-level photo-reconnaissance. While these exercises were still in progress the carrier HMS *Albion* also sailed for the Mediterranean following a refit; she arrived at the end of August and began working up her squadrons of Sea Hawks and Sea Venoms. En route to Malta she passed *Ocean* and *Theseus*, homeward bound once more after their initial period of trooping. On their return to the UK both carriers were provided with more permanent accommodation for further trooping work: *Ocean* was fitted with an operating theatre and extensive hospital facilities, which would enable her to be used as a hospital ship on station off the Egyptian coast during the operation.

This re-equipment had hardly been completed when both ships were suddenly assigned a new role as helicopter carriers. HMS *Ocean* was to embark the Whirlwinds of No 845 Squadron, while *Theseus* was to take on the mixed complement of Sycamores and Whirlwinds belonging to the Joint Experimental Helicopter Unit (JEHU), a combined Army and RAF venture. This meant that many of the bunks newly erected in the carriers' hangars had to be taken out again.

On 30 September, both carriers put to sea to practise helicopter operation techniques. Fourteen days later, No 845 Squadron was transferred from *Ocean* to *Theseus* in place of the JEHU aircraft, and the carrier sailed for Malta. Five days afterwards, *Ocean* also sailed for the Mediterranean after embarking JEHU.

In Malta, the men of No 45 Commando had been anticipating a helicopter assault in which a commando task force was to have been landed by two waves of No 845 Squadron's helicopters to secure the strategic bridges to the south of Port Said, on 27 October. However, this mission was assigned to the French paratroops, and the Commandos' mission was now to act as helicopter reserve to the main seaborne assault in the first phase of the operation, standing ready to support Nos 40 and 42 Commandos at any point on the beachhead as required.

In Cyprus, the 16th Parachute Brigade Group was being brought up to strength by an influx of reservists. On the arrival of the 2nd Battalion in September, the 1st and 3rd Battalions – which had been conducting anti-terrorist operations – were flown back to the United Kingdom for refresher parachute training, following which they returned to Cyprus in the Middle of October.

The French, for their part, had already been in Cyprus for some weeks, the initial contingent of 2,700 men of the 10th Parachute Division arriving at Limassol on 7 September. The majority were billeted in a collection of huts and tents known as 'Camp X' at Tymbou, where they soon became the target of EOKA propaganda. The terrorists scattered leaflets around the French area, exhorting the Paras to abandon co-operation with the British and hand over their weapons to EOKA. The paratroops' experience in Algeria had not made them well disposed to terrorists, and on several ocasions they opened fire on EOKA agents who revealed themselves.

EOKA had no inkling that military and political collusion leading up to the forthcoming operation was more than just an Anglo-French affair. Involved also was the State of Israel, a fact that was to remain one of *Musketeer*'s best-kept secrets for many years.

CHAPTER FOUR

THE ISRAELI CONNECTION

In September 1956, with the prospect of a diplomatic solution
to the Suez crisis still a possibility, the focus of attention in the
Middle East suddenly shifted to Jordan. Racked by internal
problems, Jordan now found itself facing the possibility of
armed conflict with Israel, and if that happened, Britain
– which had a long-standing treaty with Jordan, guaranteeing
military assistance against aggression in exchange for the use
by the RAF of two Jordanian airfields, Amman and Mafraq –
would almost certainly become embroiled. In fact, the British
had a war plan, code-named Operation *Cordage*, to cover just
such an eventuality.

For several months the Israelis had put up with terrorist
infiltration from Jordan; 29 Israelis had been killed and 33 injured
as a result of such activities during the six-month period up to
the end of August 1956. Then, on 10 September, an untrained
Israeli Army unit on a map-reading exercise in the vicinity of
the border was fired on by the Jordanian National Guard. Six
Israelis were killed and three wounded. While the incident was
being investigated by the Mixed Armistice Commission, an
Israeli battalion crossed the Jordanian frontier west of Hebron
on the following night, attacked the police fort at Rahwah, killed
six policemen and ten soldiers, and then blew up the building,
together with a UN school nearby. An Arab Legion patrol
hurrying up to reinforce was ambushed, another four soldiers
being killed and three wounded. On the night of 13/14 September
Israeli troops attacked another police post at Gharandal, killing
eight Jordanians and wounding several more.

The Foreign Office repeated earlier warnings to Israel that
Britain would stand by the Anglo-Jordan Treaty, and maintained

air and naval units that would be used in support of Jordan in a state of readiness. The Venoms of No 249 (Gold Coast) Squadron, the 'resident' RAF strike squadron at Amman, had been redeployed to Cyprus in late August as part of the Suez Task Force buildup, but its place had been taken by No 32 Squadron from Malta, also armed with the Venom. Other British forces in the country were a light anti-aircraft wing of the RAF Regiment, an armoured regiment and an infantry company. Because of the Suez crisis the Jordanians indicated that more British ground reinforcements would not be welcome, and instead turned to Iraq to discuss the possible entry of Iraqi troops into Jordan.

The Jordanians were expecting the Israelis to mount a major attack, and they accordingly withdrew their fighting troops of the Arab Legion back from the frontier and formed them into tactical groups, leaving the border posts manned by the far less disciplined National Guard. It was one of these militia who, on 23 September, opened fire on a group of archaeologists on the Israeli side of the border, killing four and wounding sixteen. There were two more incidents on the following day, involving the deaths of two more Israeli civilians, and on 25 September the Israeli Prime Minister, David Ben-Gurion, called a special Cabinet meeting to decide on military action against the Arab Legion by way of retaliation.

The question of major reprisals had to be considered with great care in the light of recent diplomatic developments. At the heart of these was Shimon Peres, then Director-General of the Israeli Defence Ministry, who had been carefully consolidating links between the French and Israeli defence organisations ever since negotiations for the acquisition of French arms began in 1954. Peres already knew that the French had considered including Israel in the overall plan for armed operations against Egypt, especially as a contingency in the event that Britain should prove reluctant to launch an attack; moreover, the French were prepared to work with the Israelis as equals, an important point for a small nation beset by enemies and desperate to cultivate international recognition.

Peres flew back to Israel from Paris on the eve of the emergency Cabinet meeting with this news. Ben-Gurion's immediate reaction was that this was the birth of the first serious alliance between Israel and a Western power, and that Israel must accept it. According to Peres, Ben-Gurion was anxious to avoid a war with Britain over Jordan, which might disrupt his country's increasingly promising relations with France; therefore, although he would not abandon his policy of reprisal against the Jordanians, any such reprisal would have to be limited to the extent that it would be unlikely to provoke Britain into military action under the terms of the Anglo-Jordan Treaty. He accordingly authorised an attack on the Arab Legion post at Husan, in the Jerusalem hills near where the previous incidents had taken place.

Meanwhile, Ben-Gurion also appointed a delegation to go to Paris, at the invitation of the French, to take part in discussions on possible active military collaboration. The delegation consisted of Golda Meir and Moshe Carmel, a former general, Shimon Peres and General Moshe Dayan, the Israeli Chief of Staff. Their brief was to point out to the French that the Israeli forces would not be 100 per cent ready by 15 October, the date on which the French had indicated they wished to launch the Suez operation; also, the Israelis needed to know that the undertaking had the active backing of Britain and would be implemented with the knowledge of the United States. Israel's war aims would be to obtain control of the west coast of the Gulf of Aqaba and the entrance into the Straits of Tiran at Sharm-el-Sheikh, so opening the way to the development of Eilat as a major seaport.

During the night of 25/26 September the Israelis launched their planned reprisal attack on Husan, which did not go as planned. The Arab Legion resisted fiercely and the border post was only destroyed after bloody hand-to-hand fighting that cost the lives of ten Israelis, with sixteen more wounded. Thirty-seven Jordanian troops and police were killed, together with two civilians, and eleven were wounded.

The meeting between French and Israeli civil and military leaders took place in Montparnasse, Paris, on 30 September/1 October. It quickly emerged that the French wanted the Israelis to attack first, giving the French and British a pretext for joining in later. However, Ben-Gurion's brief to his delegation had made the inflexible point that the Allies must attack simultaneously.

The French stressed that it was vital to move quickly for a

35

variety of reasons. If Anthony Eden should submit to political pressure and the British Government decided against offensive action, the French and Israelis would need to act decisively before the onset of bad weather in the eastern Mediterranean. Also, the Americans were preoccupied with forthcoming presidential elections; President Eisenhower would hardly impose sanctions against Israel and risk losing the Jewish vote. In any case, as General Maurice Challe – a French Air Force officer present at the talks – pointed out, American officers at NATO Headquarters near Paris were already actively conniving at French action in that they had agreed to release military equipment (mostly spares for the F-84Fs) deployed to Cyprus.

Clearly, it would be beneficial to both French and Israelis if Britain threw her full military weight into the venture. The first priority would be the elimination of the Egyptian Air Force through the destruction of its airfields, and the aircraft best suited to this task were the RAF's Canberras and Valiants, or so the French believed. The Royal Navy, too, could throw a formidable amount of air power into the air support phase of the operation, the Fleet Air Arm adding its ground-attack muscle to that of the RAF and FAF fighter-bombers on Cyprus. The Cyprus base was crucial to the operation, too; France had no others in the area. Moreover, joint Anglo-French planning for the operation was proceeding well; for a wedge to be driven through the middle of it by Britain's sudden withdrawal would be highly counter-productive.

The two days of talks (which the Israelis called the Conference of St Germain, after the district where their delegation was housed) set the seal on the delivery of more military equipment from France, including Super-Sherman tanks, tank transporters, bazookas and trucks with four-wheel drive to negotiate the rugged terrain of the Sinai desert. The delegation returned home leaving the French impressed by Moshe Dayan's complete confidence that his forces could take Sinai quickly, even without allies. A French military mission led by General Maurice Challe, which returned to Israel with the delegation to assess the military capability of the Israeli armed forces and to discuss the possibility of basing French air units in Israel if the British did not join in and Cyprus became unavailable, was less impressed by what it saw.

The Israeli Army appeared scruffy and ill-disciplined, and much of its equipment was the result of on-the-spot improvisation. One French officer, gazing at what he took to be a tribe of gypsies, discovered to his amazement that they were Army reservists, heading for their base after being called up. Nevertheless, Moshe Dayan succeeded in overcoming French scepticism, and in convincing General Challe that the Israelis would not only fight but also achieve their objectives in Sinai in the allotted time, ambitious though the overall plan might seem. The plan now had a name: Operation *Kadesh*.

On 4 October, while the French mission was still in Israel, two vehicles were ambushed in broad daylight by a party of Arab terrorists on the Beersheba road, nine miles inside Israeli territory. With the UN Security Council in session, Ben-Gurion decided not to initiate immediate reprisals; the outcome of the UN talks would decide whether or not Britain and France would go to war with Egypt. Five days later, however, two Israeli labourers were murdered and mutilated in an orange grove between Tel Aviv and Haifa, and Ben-Gurion authorised a reprisal attack on the police fort outside the Jordanian town of Qalqilya. On this occasion, the raid – which was mounted on the night of 10/11 October – was preceded by an artillery bombardment, and Israeli aircraft cruised overhead. The attack on the police fort was successful, but a unit sent out to ambush Arab Legion reinforcements ran into trouble and suffered heavy casualties, the survivors being extricated across the border only with great difficulty after daybreak.

It was at this point that a situation developed that might have brought Britain and Israel into armed conflict with one another. While the raid was still in progress, King Hussein invoked the Anglo-Jordan Treaty and called for assistance from the RAF units stationed in the country. At 04.15 on 11 October, the British Consul-General in Jerusalem telephoned the Israeli Governor of the city and warned him that, if the Israeli attack was not called off immediately, there was grave danger of Britain and Israel finding themselves at war. Later in the morning, King Hussein summoned the British Ambassador, told him that a major Israeli attack appeared imminent, and asked for all the British help possible, including the immediate reinforcement of the RAF contingent in Jordan. The immediate British response, initiated by the Foreign Office on 12 October, was to despatch flights of Hawker Hunter fighters from Cyprus to Amman; these aircraft did not remain in Jordan for long, but returned to Cyprus after spending a few hours on the ground.

Also on 12 October, the British Embassy informed the Israelis that units of the Iraqi army were about to enter Jordan and would remain stationed there indefinitely. In fact, King Hussein had cabled his cousin, King Faisal, and asked him to send a division immediately. The Israelis viewed this development with alarm, seeing it as a direct threat to their country's security, and hinted that they might be prepared to take military action to forestall it; this compelled Peter Westlake, the British Chargé d'Affaires in Tel Aviv, to tell the Israelis firmly that any military move to counter the entry of Iraqi forces into Jordan would activate the Anglo-Jordan alliance. He left them in no doubt that, under such circumstances, the RAF would bomb Israeli territory.

There were different views in Whitehall, where Jordan's predicament was being viewed less sympathetically. Britain's military chiefs knew full well that if the Israelis went on the offensive in Jordan, they would quickly destroy the Jordanian army and occupy the country, and neither the Iraqis nor any action by the RAF would stop them. The Jordanian Government was harbouring a dangerous illusion that the RAF's striking power could win a war for them; what was likely to happen, if the RAF attacked targets in Israel, was that the Israelis would attack the British bases in Cyprus, which, to say the least, would be highly inconvenient at this juncture. General Sir Gerald Templer, the Chief of the Imperial General Staff, summed up the situation bluntly and fairly: he told Ministers that Britain could either go to the aid of Jordan against Israel with sea and air power or it could launch *Musketeer*. Britain could not do both. The First Sea Lord, Admiral Mountbatten, also pointed out that there was the reaction of the United States to be considered.[4] 'If, during *Musketeer*, Israel attacked Jordan and the US went to Jordan's aid against Israel, then we and the US would be fighting on opposite sides. We should be the unwilling allies of Israel and our forces in Jordan would be hostages to fortune.'

On Sunday, 14 October, an Iraqi military delegation arrived

in Amman to discuss the entry of Arab troops into Jordan. On that same day, Anthony Eden entertained two distinguished French guests at Chequers: Albert Gazier, the French Minister for Social Affairs, and General Maurice Challe. It was the latter, newly converted to the idea of a swift Israeli victory in Sinai, who came up with a possible solution to the dilemma, one that would divert Israeli attention from events in Jordan. The Israelis, he suggested, should be encouraged to launch an attack against Egyptian forces in Sinai and to occupy the whole of the peninsula up to the line of the Canal. Britain and France could then issue an ultimatum to both sides, ordering them to withdraw their forces from the area of the Canal so as to avoid damage to it. The British and French could then send in their own forces to separate the combatants and to occupy the whole length of the Canal from Port Said to Suez. Challe mentioned the possibility of a simultaneous seaborne landing at Port Said and paratroop drops at other key points, such as Ismailia.

Challe had almost certainly already discussed this scheme with Moshe Dayan. Israel's political leaders were unaware of it, and it was not until 16 October that it was presented to Ben-Gurion. Eden liked the plan, but would not commit his support to it until discussions with key people had taken place. Meanwhile, efforts were to be made to persuade the Iraqis to delay their move into Jordan for at least 48 hours.

There was one matter of serious concern to Ben-Gurion, and that was the possibility that Israel's cities might come under heavy Egyptian air attack while the Israeli Air Force was supporting the offensive in Sinai. General Challe, visiting Israel again on 21 October, put forward the reassurance that the necessary air defence would be provided by French fighters based in Israel.

That same day, Ben-Gurion flew to Paris on Challe's aircraft. He was accompanied by Moshe Dayan, Shimon Peres, and Colonel Mordechai Bar-On, the head of Dayan's office. In strict secrecy, the delegation was taken to a villa in the Parisian suburb of Sevres, where they met the French Prime Minister, Guy Mollet, the Foreign Minister, Christian Pineau, and the Minister of Defence, Maurice Bourges-Maunoury. By the time the British delegation arrived, a preliminary plan for joint action had already been discussed.

The British representatives were Selwyn Lloyd, the Foreign Secretary, and his junior private secretary, Donald Logan. After being briefed by Pineau, Selwyn Lloyd was taken in to meet the Israelis. The atmosphere was less than cordial; there was a distinct barrier, amounting almost to antagonism, between Ben-Gurion and Lloyd, and for a time the French were concerned that the talks might fall apart. At length, however, the details of tripartite collusion were agreed, and on 24 October it was formalised by the signing, in the deepest secrecy, of the document called the 'Protocol of Sevres'. The Israeli attack would take place on 28 October, and the British and French would subsequently intervene as self-appointed peacekeepers to separate the combatants. The Israelis would accept their ultimatum and withdraw ten miles from the Canal. It was assumed that Nasser would reject the ultimatum; the Israelis were given the impression that in this event the Allies would begin bombing Egypt at first light on 31 October.

Anthony Eden hoped and expected that the secret of this collusion would never be revealed. He was furious to learn that an actual piece of paper had been drawn up. All copies of the British version were destroyed, but the Israeli version of the 'Protocol of Sevres' was preserved, and still is. But the really important aspect of the deceit was that every military move made by the Allies thereafter was constrained by the need to conserve the secret. The British and French were coming to Egypt, but to have had their invasion fleet in sight on the horizon at the very moment the Israelis launched their attack would have been too much of a coincidence in the eyes of the world.

CHAPTER FIVE

THE EGYPTIAN FORCES

Throughout the military planning for *Musketeer*, a major worry was the reaction that might come from the Eastern Bloc personnel who were training Nasser's armed forces in the use of their newly delivered Soviet equipment. The state of the Egyptian Air Force, which was continuing to receive MiG-15 jet fighters and Il-28 jet bombers, was of particular concern.

The Egyptian Air Force possessed some very fine airfields, evacuated by the RAF soon after they had been modernised for the operation of jet aircraft. The largest was Abu Sueir, ten miles west of Ismailia on the main Cairo road. The last RAF unit, No 13 Squadron (Meteor PR.10s) had left for Akrotiri in Cyprus on 10 March 1956, and less than a month later the first MiG-15s had moved in. Although Abu Sueir was used mainly as a storage depot for complete aircraft until sufficient crews had been trained to fly them, an operational MiG-15 squadron – No 30, with fifteen aircraft – had formed there in June 1956. By the middle of October 1956, Abu Sueir, according to Allied intelligence estimates, had a complement of 35 MiGs.

Another first-line base of importance was Kabrit, at the southernmost point of the Great Bitter Lake. Immediately after the RAF moved out, the Egyptians set to work lengthening the base's 6,000-foot main runway by an extra 3,000 feet to make it suitable for fast jet operation. When this work was completed, Kabrit was used as a base for the EAF's MiG-15 operational conversion unit, which shared the base with two operational MiG squadrons, Nos 1 and 20, giving a combined total of 31 aircraft. The task of these squadrons, together with No 30 at Abu Sueir, was to provide fighter cover over the Canal Zone; both bases were defended by Czech-built 20mm anti-aircraft batteries.

Fayid and Kasfareet, further to the north-west, were used by the EAF's Vampire and Meteor squadrons. Fayid was the home of No 2 Squadron, with fifteen Vampires; No 5, with twelve Meteors (F.4s and F.8s); and No 40, with twenty Vampires and ten Meteors, six of the latter tropicalised NF.13s. The EAF's remaining Vampire squadron, No 31, was based on Kasfareet. Egypt had received an initial batch of ex-RAF Vampire FB.5s in December 1949, and deliveries of FB.5s/52s continued until March 1956, by which time 62 aircraft were on the EAF inventory. Phasing out of the Vampire began when the first MiG-15s were delivered, but 44 were still in first-line service in October 1956. Five Vampires were donated to Jordan as a result of a visit to that country by the Egyptian Army's Commander-in-Chief on 14 October.

Further inland, Cairo West served as the main EAF bomber base, and in October 1956 sixteen Il-28 jet bombers were deployed there with Nos 8 and 9 Squadrons. Ten more were deployed at Almaza, the other military airfield in the vicinity of Cairo, and 22 at Luxor, in the south, although these aircraft had not yet been allocated to operational squadrons. Almaza was also the EAF's transport base, being the home of No 3 Squadron with twenty Ilyushin Il-14s, No 7 with twenty C-46 Commandos, and No 11 with twenty Dakotas. The EAF's recently acquired Meteor NF.13 night-fighters were also based there, operational with No 10 Squadron, as were eight elderly Hawker Fury piston-engined fighters.

As for the Egyptian Army, although it was reasonably well equipped, it was of dubious value as a fighting force. Despite a large-scale reorganisation programme and determined efforts to imbue an *esprit de corps*, morale remained generally low; there was still a noticeable hangover from the defeats suffered during the Arab-Israeli war of 1948-49, and corruption at senior officer level resulted in a good deal of disaffection lower down.

The Army, commanded by General Ali Ali Amer, had a mobilised strength of 100,000. It was grouped into two main formations: one for the defence of Sinai and the Gaza Strip, the other for the defence of the Canal Zone in the event of possible aggressive action on the part of Britain and France. By far the bulk of the forces were in Sinai; they included the

3rd Infantry Division, the 8th Palestinian Division and the 2nd Motorised Border Battalion. The defence of the Canal Zone was in the hands of the 2nd Infantry Division, with the 1st Armoured Brigade Team in reserve.

In all there were eighteen brigades: ten infantry, one medium machine gun, three armoured, one coastal defence and three anti-aircraft. Each of the infantry brigades, which were generally organised on British lines, was supported by an artillery battery of either British 25-pounder or Soviet 122 mm guns. An anti-tank company equipped with 17-pounder or 57 mm guns was also attached. Other artillery support was provided by independent field regiments using Soviet SU-100 self-propelled guns, or medium regiments with Soviet 152 mm guns. There were also four heavy mortar regiments – three of them deployed in Sinai – each with three batteries of 120 mm mortars.

The three armoured brigades each consisted of one armoured regiment composed of three battle groups, together with three squadrons of motorised infantry carried in either Ford Power trucks, Valentine armoured personnel carriers or Soviet BTR-152 scout cars. The armoured regiments were equipped with Soviet T-34s and JS-3s, or with British Centurion Mk 3s. A few units still used Shermans, although these were being rapidly replaced by Russian equipment.

The anti-aircraft brigades were probably the most efficient of all Egyptian Army formations, and appeared to enjoy a far higher standard of morale than other units. They were well equipped, too, with Czech-built long-barrel 20 mm cannon, 30 mm Hispano and 40 mm Bofors light AA guns, and a few Russian 57 mm cannon. The anti-aircraft batteries were deployed on airfields, at strategic points in the Canal Zone, at the entrance to the Canal itself and on the mole at Port Said. Some 20 mm batteries were sited on the roofs of buildings adjacent to depots and barracks.

Backing up the regular army was a 100,000-strong volunteer National Guard. Its standard of training was poor and its weapons outdated, consisting mainly of early models of the Lee Enfield .303 rifle. The regular army, in contrast, was equipped with the modern Soviet 7.62 mm carbine. Most of the National Guard units were mobilised late in July, and some were attached to the army in Sinai.

In addition to the National Guard there was a strong police force, run with strict military discipline, armed with the latest infantry weapons and known to be completely loyal to Nasser. During the late summer of 1956 police units received special training in street fighting and anti-paratroop operations, and it seemed likely that determined resistance would be encountered from this quarter.

Of the three Egyptian services, the Navy seemed least likely to present an obstacle to a successful invasion. Its largest warships were four destroyers, two of which – the *El Fateh* and *El Qaher* (formerly HMS *Zenith* and HMS *Myngs*) – had been refitting in England when Nasser announced the nationalisation of the Canal in July. When the British embargo on the supply of arms was announced on 30 July, the *El Qaher* was in Portsmouth making ready to sail for her home country and the *El Fateh* was undergoing trials at the Thorneycroft shipyard in Southampton. Both vessels eventually sailed for Alexandria in August, but without ammunition and torpedoes. The other two Egyptian destroyers, the *Al Nasser* and *Al Zafr*, were both ex-Soviet Skoryii-class vessels; they had been handed over to the Egyptian Navy at Alexandria on 11 June 1956.

The Navy's inventry included seven escorts: the *Tarik, Rashid, Port Said, Abikir, Domiat, El Sudan*, and *Ibrahim el Awal*, all of them ex-British. There were two former Bangor-class corvettes, the *Matrouh* and *Nasr*, and eight old wooden coastal minesweepers.

If the Egyptian Navy was in a position to present any threat at all to the Allied invasion convoys, it was likely to come from its small force of motor torpedo boats. In April 1956, twelve Soviet P-6 type MTBs had been delivered, as had two ex-Yugoslavian boats. There were also five ex-British Fairmile-type MTBs. The Soviet boats were certainly fast and armed well enough to cause problems for the Allies should the Egyptians decide to send them into action. The Egyptians were also known to have a small force of frogmen, some of whom had been trained by the Royal Navy. It was conceivable that they might operate against the Allied invasion fleet in Alexandria and Port Said, even after an official Egyptian surrender.

With all factors considered, it seemed likely to the Allied planners that, in view of the general low state of the Egyptian armed forces, even co-ordinated resistance would not last for long. The real problems could be expected to begin during the subsequent occupation phase, when the Anglo-French forces – as well as having to contend with the daily administration of a large civilian population – might also have to deal with armed terrorist groups.

Oddly enough, as September gave way to October, there seemed to be a general relaxation in the tension that had hung over the Middle East since Nasser's speech in July. Even when the Egyptian Government ordered 500 non-Egyptian employees of the Suez Canal Company to cease work – a move that had the immediate effect of halving the strength of the Canal pilots – the Canal itself continued to function and sea traffic went on flowing through it as it had always done. As time went by, the possibility that the British and French would take military action seemed increasingly remote to both the Egyptian Government and the civil population.

Even the Egyptian force in Sinai seemed affected by the apparent easing of tension; border incidents over the past weeks had been confined to skirmishes between Israel and Jordan. The Egyptians went about their routine duties as usual on Sunday 28 October, unaware that in Tel Aviv David Ben-Gurion had declared general mobilisation and that the Israeli forces were poised to strike.

Chapter Six

Operation Kadesh

Operation *Kadesh*, the Israeli plan for the offensive in Sinai, underwent some last-minute changes before it was implemented. The most important was the switch of Colonel Ariel Sharon's 202 Parachute Brigade from its original task of capturing El Arish and Sharm-el-Sheikh to securing the Mitla Pass, 40 miles east of Port Suez, and opening the way to the Suez Canal. The Israeli Air Force, whose commanders had wanted to mount a pre-emptive strike on key Egyptian air bases, were now firmly ordered not to cross the Canal.

In the days before the offensive, twenty F-84Fs of the *1ere Escadre* and sixteen Mystere IVs of the *2eme Escadre* were deployed to Israel to form a Wing under the command of Colonel Maurice Perdrizet, who had been a senior planner in London. Air Chief Marshal Sir Denis Smallwood remembers that Perdrizet was[5]

> sent for one morning by his boss, General Brohan. After a short time he returned looking very pale. When I asked him what the problem was he said that he had to leave immediately. 'Where to?' I asked. 'I cannot say.' 'For how long?' He couldn't tell me. 'When will you return?' 'To this place, never.' When we had eventually moved out to Cyprus I was rung up by the Wing Commander (Ops) at Akrotiri. He said that a French F-84 Wing had just landed to refuel and after a rapid turnaround they had taken off and disappeared off the radar to the east. What was he to do about it? All I could think of was 'Just keep your bloody mouth shut!'

Operation *Kadesh* was preceded by an extraordinary operation reminiscent of the time in 1943 when American P-38 fighters shot

46

down in the Pacific the aircraft carrying the Japanese supremo, Admiral Yamamoto. On the night of 28/29 October, the pilot of an Israeli Meteor was briefed to intercept an Egyptian Ilyushin Il-14 transport over the Mediterranean and shoot it down. The aircraft, bound from Damascus to Cairo, was thought by Israeli Intelligence to be carrying the Egyptian Commander-in-Chief, General Abdul Hakim Amer, who had been visiting the Syrians to put the finishing touches to a plan for an alliance against Israel's expected attack on Jordan. In fact Amer was not on the aircraft, having delayed his departure until the next day, but eighteen of his senior staff officers were killed when the Il-14 was destroyed.

The Israeli attack on the Egyptian forces in Sinai began at 16.30 on 29 October with the airdrop of 395 men of the 1st Battalion, 202 Airborne Brigade, by sixteen C-47s of the IAF's No 301 Squadron. Close escort was provided by ten Meteor Mk 8s, and high cover by twelve Mystéres. The remainder of the Brigade, some 2,000 men spearheaded by two companies mounted in French 6x6 trucks with front-wheel drive, had already crossed the start line on the first stage of the 130-mile dash to Mitla, making a diversionary feint towards the Jordanian frontier. Two hundred of these indispensable trucks had arrived in Israel just in time, half being assigned to the paratroop brigade and the rest to 9 Brigade, which was to attack Sharm-el-Sheikh.

The airdrop did not go entirely to plan, the paratroops landing about three miles east of the Dropping Zone and suffering 13 casualties. After a two-hour march the men reached their objective, the Parker Memorial (a monument to Colonel Parker, the British officer who was twice governor of Sinai) at the eastern end of the Mitla Pass and began to dig themselves in, setting up roadblocks and clearing a DZ to the east. At 21.00 Nord Noratlas transports of the French Air Force's *64eme Escadre*, operating from Haifa, dropped eight jeeps, four 116 mm recoilless guns, two 20 mm mortars, ammunition and food.

Meanwhile, the main body of the Airborne Brigade had overrun the frontier post at Kuntilla, but problems with the Brigade's requisitioned transport, much of which was in a sorry state, led to a five-hour delay before the men were able to push on to their next objective, the fortified post at El Thamad, forty miles further on. This was defended by two companies of the Egyptian Frontier Force and a National Guard detachment, the Egyptians putting up a spirited resistance before they were overwhelmed at the cost of sixty dead shortly after sunrise on 30 October. Israeli losses were three killed and ten wounded, although forty more casualties were inflicted by four MiG-15s that strafed the 2nd Battalion, now occupying the former Egyptian positions, at about 07.00.

The next objective was Nakhl, another forty miles to the west, but the Israeli brigade commander was faced with a dilemma. Although an airdrop by Noratlases brought welcome supplies, and his supporting artillery – which had become bogged down on the drive from Kuntilla – turned up shortly before noon, his column would present an excellent target for Egyptian fighter-bombers as it pushed on in broad daylight. The damaging attack by the MiG-15s had left him with little confidence that the Israeli Air Force could keep all the enemy aircraft at bay; the other alternative was to disperse the Brigade and wait until nightfall before resuming the advance. Much depended on how the 1st Battalion was faring.

In fact, it was not faring very well, having been under attack since dawn by Egyptian forces that had been rushed up to occupy high ground on the southern side of the Mitla Pass. The Israeli positions were being heavily mortared, and although a probing attack had been beaten off by the paratroops it could only be a matter of time before a heavier assault developed. Units of the Egyptian 2 Brigade were already crossing the Canal and forming up in preparation for a drive to Mitla.

During the morning the paratroops were attacked several times by MiG-15s and Vampire FB.52s, which caused some casualties and destroyed a Piper Cub liaison aircraft that had been sent from El Thamad to find out what was happening. A second Cub escaped the strafing attacks and returned with the necessary intelligence. As a result of this the Airborne Brigade commander was informed by GHQ that air support would be available from 13.00 onwards. Fighter cover was now to be provided by the French Mysteres and F-84Fs, leaving the Israeli Ouragans, Meteors and Mysteres free for ground attack missions.

The Brigade commander requested immediate air cover for the battalion at Mitla and air support for the follow-on column on the drive to Nakhl from 16.00. The main body of the brigade moved off at 13.30, with air cover, and no further attacks were made on it by the EAF during this phase. Nakhl was reached at 16.00 and the assault began almost immediately, supported by artillery and French-built AMX tanks. The main defensive position was overrun after half an hour and by nightfall the whole area was in Israeli hands. Leaving one battalion at Nakhl, the Brigade pressed on to Mitla under cover of darkness. The drive was not opposed and the link-up with the men of the 1st Battalion was made at 22.30. Supply drops were made by Dakotas and Noratlases and the Airborne Brigade dug itself in and prepared to withstand the expected Egyptian counter-attack.

In fact, the movement of the Egyptian 2 Brigade from the Canal had been hampered by the Israeli Air Force, in almost constant action since 14.00 on 30 October. Twenty IAF F-51 Mustangs attacked enemy columns on the east bank of the Canal with bombs and rockets and also provided support for the Israeli Central Task Force's assault on Kuseima, where some of the heaviest fighting of the initial phase of the campaign was taking place. Two of the Mustangs were lost to ground fire.

During the first day the EAF flew about 40 sorties, the last attack being carried out on the Mitla positions by two Meteors escorted by MiGs. Meanwhile, eight Mysteres engaged twelve MiGs over the east bank of the Canal, the IAF pilots claiming two MiGs destroyed and two probables. One Mystere was badly damaged, but the pilot flew it back to base and made a safe landing.

By midnight on 30 October, two more Egyptian battalions had reached Mitla, and the bulk of the 2nd Armoured Brigade had crossed the Canal and was preparing to move forward. It seemed that the Egyptians were recovering well from the initial shock of the Israeli offensive. The next morning, the Central Task Force became involved in more heavy fighting, its 7th Armoured Brigade, which had circled Abu Agheila in north-eastern Sinai, coming under heavy fire from Egyptian artillery positions at Um Shihan. Two Egyptian armoured attacks by T-34s were beaten off by anti-tank guns and wire-guided Nord SS-10 missiles – the first time that guided weapons were used against tanks – and a third by air support.

On the morning of D+2 an IAF Harvard reconnaissance aircraft reported large Egyptian reinforcements, including armour, driving eastwards through El Hama, only twenty-five miles west of Abu Agheila. The Israeli brigade commander at once ordered two companies of infantry and a squadron of Sherman tanks to set up a road block fifteen miles to the west, and requested air support. This arrived in the shape of four Ouragans, but these were bounced by eight MiG-15s, which had been flying top cover for four Meteors attacking Israeli units south-east of El Hama, and were only rescued by the timely arrival of some Mysteres. All the Ouragans were damaged in the combat.

In fact, the IAF reconnaissance pilot had made a mistake and the Egyptian column was not at El Hama but at Bir Gifgafa, a good fifty miles from Abu Agheila. Once the correct location had been established another flight of Ouragans was sent out to attack it, but once again their mission was frustrated by the appearance of MiGs, one of which was shot down. The IAF operated all day, with Ouragans and Mustangs maintaining constant pressure on the Egyptian ground forces while the Mysteres and F-84Fs flew combat air patrols. The ground-attack aircraft inflicted considerable damage on the Bir Gifgafa column, particularly on the 1st Armoured Brigade, which lost ninety tanks, trucks and personnel carriers despite being well defended by mobile 40 mm AA guns.

In the Mitla Pass, the men of the Airborne Brigade had been involved in a day of heavy fighting as they tried to dislodge the Egyptians from their positions. Throughout the day, in spite of air patrols, the Brigade had been subjected to sporadic air attacks by EAF Meteors and Vampires. One of the heaviest came at 16.00 when part of the attacking Israeli force was cut off in a defile and strafed by four Meteors, which inflicted heavy casualties. One Meteor was destroyed by CAP Mysteres.

By nightfall the Israeli paratroops had seized the high ground on both sides of the Pass, and three hours of bitter hand-to-hand fighting followed as they drove the Egyptians from the caves below. By 19.00 the paratroops were well on the way to completing their task, but they had suffered fifty men killed and three times that many wounded. After dark three C-47s flew in supplies and evacuated about 100 wounded from the DZ, the aircraft landing in the light of flares.

At the end of D+2, the key Abu Agheila position in the north-east had been captured by the Israelis, who were now preparing to launch an attack on Um Gatef. The 7th Armoured Brigade was at Bir Hasana and ready, if necessary, to reinforce the paratroops at Mitla: Rafah, the key to the Gaza Strip, was also under heavy Israeli attack. In the air, the EAF had lost three Vampires, three MiGs and two Meteors, but it had pressed home its attacks with determination.

Meanwhile, the Anglo-French ultimatum to Israel and Egypt had been issued, and as expected had been rejected by the latter in the early hours of 31 October. From 1 November, with allied air attacks on targets in Egypt having begun, the French air units in Israel were authorised to carry out offensive operations in support of the Israeli ground forces.

With the threat of invasion by Anglo-French forces now a reality, Nasser issued orders on the morning of 1 November for all Egyptian units not engaging the Israeli forces in Sinai to withdraw across the Suez Canal. The order coincided with an Israeli assault on Rafah at the southern end of the Gaza Strip, preceded by a bombardment from the destroyers *Yafo*, *Eilat* and the French cruiser *Georges Leygues*. The Egyptian positions were bombed before dawn by IAF Mosquitos, and at first light Mustangs and Ouragans attacked with rockets and napalm. The Egyptians again fought hard, but their positions were overrun one by one and at 08.00 their commander ordered a withdrawal to El Arish. This position was attacked during the afternoon by a battalion of AMX tanks with infantry and air support.

Sporadic Egyptian air attacks continued during the morning of 1 November, but by mid-afternoon this activity had virtually ceased. By this time, the main Egyptian airfields had been subjected to heavy strafing attacks by allied fighter-bombers, and it was soon apparent that an exodus of Egyptian aircraft from the threatened areas was in progress. In the early part of the afternoon, a few MiG-15s and three Meteor NF.13s were seen over Sinai, but they stayed at altitude, heading north-east, and did not offer combat.

From now on, the Israeli Air Force was free to turn its attention to ground attack operations, striking at the Egyptian forces still in position at Abu Agheila and Um Gatef. The Egyptians counter-attacked with armour after dark in an attempt to smash through a blocking force set up by the Israelis to the west of Abu Agheila, but the attack was broken up by artillery fire.

At dawn on 1 November, the men of the Airborne Brigade stood to in their positions in the Mitla Pass and waited to repel the armoured counter-attack that was expected from Gifgafa. It never came. During the late afternoon, IAF reconnaissance aircraft reported that columns of Egyptian troops and vehicles were disengaging and streaming back across the desert towards the Canal. By the following morning, it was obvious that the Egyptians in Sinai were in full retreat, their withdrawal covered by the 1st Armoured Brigade at Bir Gifgafa, which itself began to pull back in mid-morning, and a mobile brigade astride the coastal road between El Arish and Kantara. The Israelis caught up with the 1st Armoured Brigade's rearguard thirty miles from the Canal at 16.00 and knocked out three T-34s, but the bulk of the Brigade succeeded in re-crossing the Canal during the night. It had been under constant IAF attack since dawn, losing twenty-two tanks, five SU-100 SP guns and at least thirty-five personnel carriers.

At first light on 2 November the focus of air support shifted to the coast road, where the Israeli 27th Armoured Brigade was advancing rapidly towards Kantara. The Israeli troops counted four hundred Egyptian vehicles of all types and forty tanks by the roadside; some were the victims of air attack, but most had been abandoned intact.

Meanwhile, at 06.00 on 2 November, the Israeli 9th Infantry Brigade had begun an advance along the Gulf of Aqaba from Ras el Nakeb, north-west of Eilat, towards Sharm-el-Sheikh, which – together with Ras Nasrani – commanded the Straits of Tiran. While the IAF attacked Sharm-el-Sheikh during the afternoon, two companies of paratroops were dropped at El Tur and a battalion of the 12th Infantry Brigade was flown in, together with its supporting equipment.

By the end of the day, the El Tur task force was preparing to advance on Sharm-el-Sheikh and the 9th Infantry Brigade was making its way over high ground towards the same objective. A battalion of paratroops had also left the Mitla area, advancing towards Ras Sudar on the Gulf of Suez. Its objective was to link up with the task force at El Tur, completing the encirclement of the Sinai Peninsula.

At dawn on 3 November, virtually the whole of the Gaza Strip was in the hands of the Israeli 11th Infantry Brigade. In the south, the paratroop battalion reached Ras Sudar, which it captured after a short firefight, and regrouped there. The remainder of the Airborne Brigade at Mitla assembled at the western end of the Pass and prepared to advance on Port Tewfik, but this plan was cancelled and the Brigade stood ready to complete the occupation of southern Sinai. General Moshe Dayan's main concern now was to complete this task before United Nations pressure brought a halt to Israeli operations. Accordingly, in the afternoon of 3 November he ordered his forces to proceed with the capture of Sharm-el-Sheikh and Ras Nasrani with all possible speed.

The paratroop battalion reached El Tur at noon the following day and prepared for the final attack, the two companies of reserve paratroops and the infantry battalion already at El Tur being evacuated by air in the course of the day. Meanwhile, the 9th Infantry Brigade approached Ras Nasrani and called in air support, expecting to meet with stiff resistance. The Israeli pilots, to everyone's surprise, reported no anti-aircraft fire. The reason was simple enough: the Egyptians had spiked the fortress's big naval guns and fallen back on Sharm-el-Sheikh.

At 14.00 the Israeli column arrived opposite the perimeter of Sharm-el-Sheikh and came under heavy fire from an outpost. Two Mustangs were called in and saturated the post with two salvoes of 16 rockets, after which it offered no further resistance. The IAF subjected the Sharm-el-Sheikh defences to a heavy pounding during the remainder of the afternoon, but this did not prevent the Egyptians from breaking up the first Israeli ground attack, which went in at 03.30 on 5 November. At 07.00 the infantry moved forward again with air support and reached the wire on the western perimeter of their objective, where they were once again pinned down by heavy fire. For the next hour the Israelis were involved in some of the most vicious hand-to-hand fighting of the whole campaign as they blasted their way through the wire under cover of a smokescreen and stormed the Egyptian positions. Then, at 08.30, the paratroop battalion from El Tur arrived and entered the battle, and after that the defences were quickly overrun, the Egyptians surrendering at 09.00.

At 11.30, the IAF mounted its last strike mission of the campaign when Mustangs and Ouragans attacked the small island of Sanafir, adjacent to Tiran about two miles offshore. Soon afterwards Israeli troops landed there, but found the island deserted. The small Egyptian garrison had been evacuated before first light. The Sinai mission was at an end.

CHAPTER SEVEN

FINAL DEPLOYMENTS

As the Allied planning for possible military action against Egypt continued, so did the deployment of RAF and French air units to Cyprus. The early deployment of No 58 Squadron's PR Canberras, and of the Tangmere Wing's Hunters, has already been mentioned, as has the move from Jordan to Akrotiri of No 249 Squadron's Venoms under the command of Sqn Ldr J.R. Maitland. These were followed, on 5 September, by the sixteen Venoms of No 8 Squadron (Sqn Ldr C.I. Blyth DFC AFC); normally based in Aden, they were just completing Armament Practice Camp Training at Habbaniyah, in Iraq. Between 27 September and 26 October the congestion at Akrotiri was increased by the arrival, in relays, of thirty-six F-84F Thunderstreaks of the *Armée de l'Air*'s *3eme Escadre* and six RF-84F Thunderflash tactical reconnaissance aircraft of the *33eme Escadre*.

Meanwhile, the Canberra light bomber force – sixty aircraft in total – began to build up at Nicosia. The first to arrive, on 19 October, were eight Canberra B.2s of No 18 Squadron from Upwood (Sqn Ldr A.H. Chamberlain) and twelve B.6s of No 139 Squadron from Binbrook (Sqn Ldr P. Mallorie). The latter squadron – half of which was in Malta at the time, undergoing Main Force training that included taking off with full bomb and fuel loads – was intended for the marker role, as was its sister squadron at Binbrook, No 109.

Both squadrons had been cleared in 1954 to drop 250 lb target indicators, and in December 1955 their B.6s were also cleared to drop 4.5in parachute flares. Both units were Main Force squadrons and, in the face of the prevailing threat at the time, had been trained to penetrate enemy defences at high level and bomb using G-H as a navigation and aiming system. They were unique among Main Force Canberra squadrons in having no visual bombing capability, the bomb aimer's position having been removed and replaced by a sideways-looking radar called Blue Shadow, which gave the navigator a radar print of returns at 90 degrees to starboard of the aircraft, up to a distance of around sixty miles, depending on the height. The crews had gained considerable experience in the use of this equipment, although, as yet, they had received no directive about its operational employment. As Sqn Ldr Paul Mallorie, the officer commanding No 139 Squadron, said at a much later date: 'We presumed that all would be revealed when necessary and we used the equipment, partly because we had ground crew who were trained to service it, and partly because it was quite fun to use.'

The two marker squadrons had inherited a low-level, shallow-dive target marking technique from their days as Mosquito Pathfinder Force units during the Second World War. This role had now become very much a secondary one after the Mosquitos were replaced by Canberras, and the Squadrons' training programme incorporated only very infrequent visits to the Wainfleet bombing range by day, and occasionally by night. It was, quite literally, a hit-or-miss business, as Sqn Ldr Mallorie explains[6]:

> At night, it was well-lit and we dropped details of practice bombs from a theoretical 30-degree dive. In practice, we found that the steeper you went, the better the results, and we had no bomb sights and were just fortunate that there were no casualties. The navigational problem was one of distinguishing between the lights of the range, and those of the Prussian Queen, a nearby pub which had unwisely invested in a set of floodlights!

Both squadrons set about refining their target marking techniques early in 1956, mainly by improving their G-H results and qualifying crews to bomb from increasing altitudes. In March 1956, No 139 Squadron sent a detachment to Libya to develop a low-level target illumination and marking technique; the crews developed low-level navigation with the aid of their Blue Shadow radar

Canberra PR.7 WH799 was shot down by a Meteor NF13 while on a reconnaissance mission over Syria on 6 November 1956. One crew member was killed.

Canberras taxying past a line of Valettas at Nicosia.

French Paras preparing to board a Noratlas of the *64eme Escadre de Transport.*

Canberras being bombed-up on Malta prior to a raid on Egyptian targets.

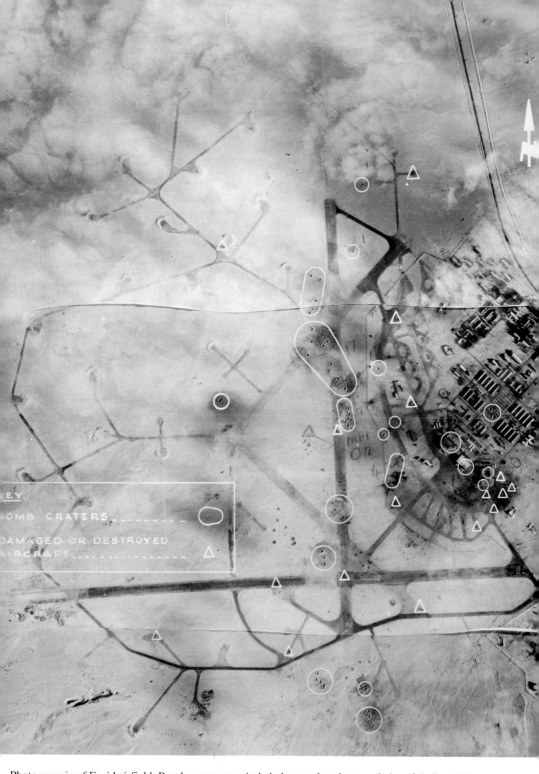

Photo-mosaic of Fayid airfield. Bomb craters are circled, damaged or destroyed aircraft indicated by a triangle.

Valiant crews being debriefed at RAF Luqa, Malta, after the first series of attacks on Egyptian airfields.

Centurion tanks of 6 RTR disembarking at Port Said.

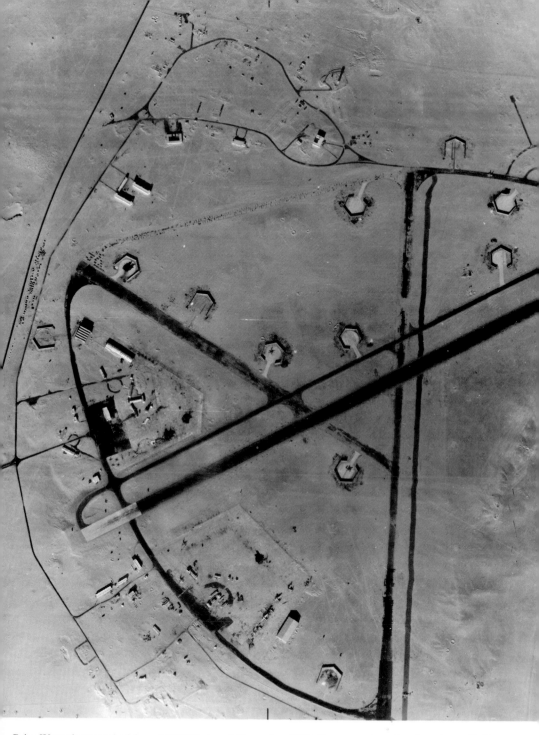

Cairo West photographed from 30,000 feet on 1 November 1956. Burnt-out aircraft and one intact Il-28 (*centre*) can be seen in the blast pens.

Cairo International airport photographed on 3 November after an attack by Valiants. As this picture shows, bombing accuracy increased as the operation progressed.

5 November 1956: British paratroops en route for the air drop at Gamil.

Sea Venom of No.893 Sqn making a belly landing on HMS *Eagle* after being damaged by flak.

The Sea Venom is hoisted off the flight deck after its successful emergency landing.

A stick of French paratroops dropping from a Nord Noratlas. The configuration of the Noratlas enabled the French to drop very compactly, as these photographs show.

equipment and arrived at a procedure involving two illuminating and two marking aircraft. This technique was modified in August, when mixed loads of flares and target indicators were approved and the four aircraft in the marking team each carried eight flares and two TIs. As an aid to navigation a third crew member was carried to map-read en route. The visual bomb sight was also replaced to give added flexibility in visual bombing from medium altitude. Also in August, No 139 Squadron took on an additional task when it provided training for Sqn Ldr Alan Chamberlain's No 18 Squadron, which was to act as a back-up marker squadron in the Suez operation.

By 26 October the remaining forty Canberras, all B.2s, had reached Nicosia. From Honington came Nos 10 (Sqn Ldr G. Sproates), 15 (Sqn Ldr A.R. Scott DFC) and 44 (Sqn Ldr J.W. Barling DSO DFC); Waddington provided No 27 Squadron (Sqn Ldr P.W. Helmore); and No 61 (Sqn Ldr N.L. Hartley) arrived from Upwood. It was the largest and most dramatic deployment of air reinforcements from the United Kingdom since World War II, and it was only part of the picture.

Early in October, the Air Staff decided that a second bomber wing was necessary to satisfy the demands of the operation, and that because of the severe overcrowding on Cyprus it would have to be based on Malta. Because of the distance of the Malta base from Egypt – about 930 miles – the Wing would comprise four squadrons of Canberra B.6s, which had a longer range than the B.2, and four squadrons of Vickers Valiants drawn from the RAF's Medium Bomber Force.

The Malta Bomber Wing, whose aircraft began to arrive at the end of September, comprised four Canberra squadrons from Binbrook: Nos 9 (Sqn Ldr L.G.A. Bastard), 12 (Sqn Ldr W.L. Donley DFC AFM), 101 (Sqn Ldr B. Moorcroft) and 109 (Sqn Ldr J.L. Causton). One of the Valiant squadron, No 138 (Wg Cdr R.G.W. Oakley DSO DFC DFM) was deployed from Wittering, while the other three were units of the Marham Wing. They were Nos 148 (Wg Cdr W.S. Burnett DSO DFC AFC), 207 (Wg Cdr D.D. Haig DSO DFC) and 214 (Wg Cdr L.H. Trent VC DFC).

By the time the deployments were completed, Malta was host to 92 bombers, of which 25 (the Valiants) were at

Luqa, 47 at Hal Far and 20 at Takali. On Cyprus there were 285 aircraft: 112 at Akrotiri, 127 at Nicosia and 46 at Tymbou. The forthcoming operation was to be controlled by three special Allied Task Forces: Naval, Military and Air. This fact did not please the Commander-in-Chief Middle East Air Force, Air Marshal H.L. Patch CB CBE, who would have preferred a single and unified command. The move deprived him and the AOC Levant, Air Vice-Marshal W.J. Crisham, of any responsibility for operations against Egypt, except for the air defence of Cyprus. The appointment of Air Marshal Barnett as Air Task Force Commander, though, was a logical one; he had recently been AOC No 205 Group in Egypt and, as one of the last officers to leave the Canal Zone, his knowledge of Egypt was up to date. For his staff, he had selected some highly experienced officers who were then undergoing the Imperial Defence College course, and who therefore did not have to be replaced in their posts.

On 23 October, Barnett and his staff set out for Cyprus in a Transport Command Comet. It was a flight that might have ended in disaster, with incalculable consequences for the operation, as Sir Denis Smallwood describes[7]:

> At roughly 45,000 feet over Crete the aeroplane went quite astonishingly silent. The first thing I noticed was that the Chief Technician rushed down to the flight deck. Within two or three minutes the Captain appeared to report to Sir Denis, dressed in his best blue. Sir Denis was reading a novel at the time, with a rather gory end to it, and he was on the last chapter and reluctant to be disturbed, but he said 'What is it?' 'We have a slight problem with the engines, Sir.' 'What sort of problem?' 'Well, we've lost all four!'
>
> It turned out to be a problem with waxing of the fuel at very low temperature, so that when we got lower down we were able to re-start engines and land at El Adem, not in Cyprus.

The combined operations rooms were based initially at Episkopi, and the build-up of the operational headquarters was complete by 30 October, the day after the Israeli offensive in Sinai began. Later, when the Task Force set sail for Port Said, the

Joint Task Force Commanders, together with some of their staffs, transferred to the headquarters ship HMS *Tyne*, where a subsidiary operations centre was set up.

Meanwhile, on 20 October, the RAF – with special Air Ministry authorisation – had flown its first reconnaissance mission over Egyptian territory. The flight was made by Flight Lieutenant G.J. Clark in Canberra PR.7 WJ821 of No 58 Squadron, who surveyed the Egyptian coastline from 30,000 feet. A fighter escort was provided by French F-84Fs, but there was no reaction. On 28 October No 13 Squadron made its first operational sortie over Egypt, and had flown four more by the end of the month. On the second sortie, on 29 October, the Canberra crewed by Sqn Ldr Field and Fg Off Lever was the target of some ineffectual Egyptian anti-aircraft fire, and the next day PR.7 WT540, flown by Flt Lt Hunter (navigator Fg Off Urquhart-Pullen) was attacked by a MiG-15 and suffered slight cannon fire damage to the elevator. Also on 30 October, Fg Off Campbell and Fg Off Toseland had a narrow escape when explosive cannon shells were seen to pass on both sides of the cockpit. Evasive action threw off the attacker, who was not identified.

On that day, all Allied aircraft involved in *Musketeer* were hastily painted with black and yellow identification stripes, General Keightley having been ordered to begin hostilities at ten hours' notice, assuming that Egypt rejected the Anglo-French ultimatum, instead of adhering to the ten-day warning period that had been envisaged. The bomber crews received their first intelligence briefings, and for many of them the selection of targets came as a surprise; they had assumed that they would be going to war against Israel.

CHAPTER EIGHT

THE NAVAL OPERATION, PHASE ONE

During the last ten days of October, the whole of the Mediterranean was a scene of intense naval activity. On the 19th, units of the French fleet slipped unobtrusively out of Toulon harbour; their crews had been told that they were heading for Bizerta, but in fact the warships rendezvoused secretly off the coast of Cyrenaica.

On the weekend of 27/28 October, troops of the 7e *Division Mecanique Rapide* embarked at Algiers and sailed for an unspecified rendezvous. In the meantime, ships of the British Mediterranean Fleet had begun to assemble off Malta for a combined naval exercise known as *Boathook*, and on the 26th the aircraft carriers HMS *Bulwark* and HMS *Eagle* sailed into Valletta harbour while HMS *Albion* stood off to sea. They had been in the vicinity of the island only a matter of hours when they received orders to sail with all speed for the eastern Mediterranean, together with the French carrier *Arromanches*. They arrived on the night of the 31st and took station some fifty miles off Port Said, in readiness for the coming series of air strikes. Their orders were to remain well to the south-west of Cyprus to avoid encroaching the operational area of the US Sixth Fleet, which at that time was well to the north. On 29 October, however, when details of the Israeli offensive became known, units of the Sixth Fleet moved south and east to provide a covering force while ships and destroyers of the Amphibious Group went into Alexandria and Haifa to evacuate US nationals. US transport aircraft also flew into Tel Aviv, Amman and Damascus for the same reason, and by 3 November the joint operation had resulted in the evacuation of 2,200 persons.

On the morning of Sunday 28 October a conference was

held between senior officers of the three British services in
Malta and orders were issued for a large-scale embarkation
exercise in war conditions. Although it was emphasised that
this was to be just another routine training exercise, most of
those present knew they were preparing for an actual military
operation.

The preparations continued throughout the 29th. The embarkation of the troops in Malta began the following morning, and
by 09.00 on the 31st the main assault force was all embarked
and ready to sail. Vessels of the Amphibious Warfare Squadron,
totalling eight LSTs and nine LCTs, carried Nos 40 and 42
Commandos and the 6th Royal Tanks, the force that was to
spearhead the seaborne assault. No 45 Commando, which was
to carry out a helicopter-borne assault, did not embark until 2
November. The main force set sail before dawn on the Wednesday
morning, escorted by warships of the Mediterranean Fleet under
the command of Rear-Admiral D.E. Holland-Martin. As soon
as the ships were at sea, the troops were informed that they were
to take part in a military action against Egypt and they were the
task force assigned to capture Port Said. After months of tedious
training, most of the men greeted the news with considerable
enthusiasm.

Meanwhile, the 3rd Infantry Division under General Churcher
was also embarking aboard troopships in the United Kingdom.
This force would still be at sea when the initial assault on Egypt
took place. Scheduled to land five days later, its task was to relieve
the assault troops and bring the campaign to an end, providing a
garrison force for the occupied areas. Still more ships carrying
supporting troops, stores and reinforcements came in the wake
of the 3rd Division.

The assault force continued on its way, the remainder of the
Mediterranean Fleet assembling behind it. Exercise *Boathook* was
now officially cancelled and the warship captains assigned new
tasks. On 30 October, the captains of HMS *Theseus* and HMS
Ocean, who had been en route to Malta to join the exercises,
were informed that their next mission would be to carry troops.
The carriers arrived in Valletta on Wednesday morning; by
Friday evening they had taken on their complement of troops,
ammunition and stores and were ready to sail. HMS *Ocean*'s

complement consisted of the Joint Experimental Helicopter Unit, 600 men of No 215 Wing, RAF Regiment, and half of No 45 Commando; HMS *Theseus* carried the rest of 45 Commando, the Whirlwind helicopters of No 845 Squadron, and support units such as engineers and administrators whose task would begin once Port Said had been occupied.

The two carriers and their escorts sailed from Malta at 17.00 on Saturday 3 November. The voyage was described by Lt Jack Smith, commanding Z Troop, No 45 Commando[8]:

> The sea passage from Malta to Port Said took three days, an intense period of briefing, rehearsal and preparation. The first day at sea was taken up with briefing and preparing loading tables. In HMS *Ocean* these were complicated because there were two types of helicopters, the Whirlwind with a load of only five fully-armed men, and the Sycamore capable of carrying three. Each man, as well as carrying his own ammunition, weapon, rations, water, respirator and spare clothing, had to carry some support weapon ammunition. All the Commando's vehicles had already sailed in the slow LST and LCT convoy a week before, and were thus unlikely to join up with the unit for some hours after landing.
>
> A loaded Sycamore presented an extraordinary sight. The back seats, side panels and unessential fittings had been stripped to increase the lift. The three passengers sat on the floor, one hunched in the middle with six mortar bombs on his lap, and the other two with their legs dangling over the side, each holding a 106 mm anti-tank shell about three feet long. The man in the centre was responsible for the two out-board members not falling out. The Whirlwind was a little more orthodox, but there were no seats, doors or windows. The five passengers hung on to any hand hold available. On approaching the landing zone the Bren gunner was ordered to put down suppressive fire out of the window if necessary, while the rifleman covered the area of the door. Communication between troops and pilot in both aircraft was either by shouting or tugging at the pilot's legs.
>
> The second day at sea was devoted to rehearsing loading

drills. The ship was darkened and the troops filed from their mess decks led by guides. The Commando was assembled in the forward hangar by helicopter sticks in landing waves. The after hangar was used for helicopter maintenance and for stowing the Joint Experimental Helicopter Unit's ground support vehicles.

The helicopters were ranged in crosses on the flight deck. On the order 'stand by' the first wave of troops was raised in the lift and led to the sponsons on the starboard side of the flight deck. Then, on 'start up', all Whirlwind motors were started. On 'emplane', the sticks were led up to their helicopters, emplaned, and the stick leader then tugged the pilot's leg, signifying that all was ready. The first wave could take off. A similar procedure was adopted to load the Sycamores.

During the third day there were further rehearsals, test firing of all automatic weapons, issues of operational ammunition, and inspections. The Commando was now ready to land.

There could be no question, however, of lifting the whole of 45 Commando in one go, as there were simply not enough helicopters available, and the two standard types were vastly different in terms both of performance and the useful load they could carry. There were two possible alternatives. The first involved sending out the helicopters in a stream, taking off from the carriers, discharging their loads individually and then returning for another load. This would help reduce congestion on the carriers' flight decks, but would not be feasible if there was strong opposition on the ground. The other alternative was for groups of helicopters to approach the landing zones in formation, discharging their cargoes at the same time, and it was felt that this was the only workable plan if there were still enemy defences to overcome. There were also other factors to be taken into consideration, which included the length of time needed to reinforce the first lift, how close the helicopters could get to the enemy defences without suffering prohibitive casualties, how many casualties might be anticipated as a result of accident or enemy action, and the effect of wind, temperature and humidity on the useful loads the helicopters could carry.

Refuelling was also going to present something of a problem, since the limited space available on the decks of *Ocean* and *Theseus* meant that only six helicopters could be refuelled at any one time. In its finalised form the helicopter assault plan called for the landing of 200 men in the first wave, with a further 170 landing in the three subsequent waves with their supporting mortars, machine-guns, anti-tank guns and ammunition. Once this assault had been completed, the tempo would be slowed down and the aim would then be to land 415 more men and 20 tons of stores in the following two and a half hours. The plan envisaged that a wave of twenty-two helicopters would need five minutes to unload its sticks of commandos and nine minutes to refuel, but in fact this time was to be reduced during the operation itself.

Both HMS *Ocean* and HMS *Theseus* were shadowed during the voyage by units of the United States Sixth Fleet, led by the heavy cruiser USS *Salem*. There was a brief exchange of signals but the American warships made no move to interfere, other than launching aircraft to keep an eye on what was happening, and contenting themselves with steaming on a parallel course. At night, however, they were a constant nuisance in that they persisted in illuminating the blacked-out vessels of the convoys with their powerful searchlights. It was a different story with the main assault force; at an early stage of the passage across the Mediterranean, one of the escorting destroyers detected an unidentified submarine in the vicinity and moved in to attack. The submarine quickly surfaced and hoisted a United States flag before sailing past the Allied ships on a reciprocal course. Other American warships steamed across the bows of the Allied convoys in an obvious attempt at harassment; on one occasion, several North American FJ-4 Furies from one of the American carriers made a series of dummy attacks on the French cruiser *Georges Leygues*, but soon sheered off when the warship's main armament swivelled round to track them. The carriers standing by to the north of Port Said also came in for some attention from the Sixth Fleet. George Black, an RAF officer on exchange with the Fleet Air Arm's No 802 Squadron (Sea Hawks, HMS *Albion*) said later[9]: 'The Sixth Fleet was a menace. It was not uncommon for aircraft to be scrambled to intercept US aircraft

64

coming to look at what was going on. This hampered operations because the carriers had to keep turning into wind to launch the intercepting aircraft, often at the most inconvenient time.'

At this stage, neither the British nor the French knew what instructions had been issued to the commander of the US Sixth Fleet. For all they knew, the Americans might even be prepared to take aggressive action to prevent the Allied convoys from reaching their destination. Later, Vice-Admiral Brown, the Sixth Fleet's commander, stated that his sole mission in the Eastern Mediterranean was to evacuate United States nationals from the combat area, and to do this he had deployed his forces in such a way as to defend the ships and aircraft from attack. Nevertheless, there was no escaping the fact that the activities of the American warships did interfere to some extent with the passage of the Allied convoys, although such actions made no difference to the schedule for the landings.

As far as the Allies were concerned, wartime conditions applied throughout the whole voyage and the ships were darkened at night. When they were not practising their drills, checking ammunition and attending lengthy briefings, the troops listened avidly to the BBC's news bulletins and to the endless political discussions, and many of them laid bets as to whether the operation would go ahead or not.

In fact, one warship – the New Zealand cruiser HMNZS *Royalist* – was withdrawn from the operation on the orders of New Zealand's Prime Minister, but the British Government had been informed in advance of his decision and the warship was replaced by the British cruiser HMS *Ceylon*, which arrived in plenty of time to take part in the operation. During the landings the cruiser's guns were to support the British paratroops on Gamil airfield, her fire directed by a small party of Royal Artillery observers who were dropped with the paratroop battalion. *Royalist*, meanwhile, remained in the Mediterranean but was ordered to take no part in any fighting, much to the disgust of the ship's company, who felt themselves humiliated and said so to the New Zealand Navy Board.

Meanwhile, on Sunday 4 November, the second echelon of the Allied invasion convoy had sailed from Cyprus. Brigadier Butler's 16th Parachute Brigade Group had been among the first to embark in their tank landing ships and the troopship *Empire Parkston*, and on Sunday morning the vessels formed up in a convoy two miles off Limassol harbour. Now that the operation was finally underway, speed was of the utmost importance and embarkation had to be carried out to a strict schedule. The men were issued with two days' rations, which had to sustain them after the landing. Personal equipment was stacked below and heavy equipment lashed to the decks. Operational briefings began even before the ships left their Cypriot harbours and were to continue throughout the whole voyage until every man knew, down to the last detail, what he had to do.

There were many of last-minute changes to the loading lists, some items being replaced by others that, it was thought, would be more appropriate. The whole process of loading was further complicated by the limited quay space of the Famagusta docks, where most of the heavy equipment went on board. Some of the merchantmen hired for the operation were in a sadly antiquated state: their loading equipment was completely inefficient and they were generally unsuited to a military operation. The brunt of the loading operation had to be borne by the Army's Z Craft, and although their crews worked non-stop it was a slow process. The loading of the troops and their first-line supporting equipment went off fairly smoothly, but after that the system began to break down. By dusk on Sunday, the whole procedure had become hopelessly entangled and it was not until the middle of the following morning that the loading schedule could be reorganised. This breakdown, together with delays in entering Port Said harbour, resulted in the stores destined for the 16th Parachute Brigade arriving in Egypt exactly three and a half hours before the paratroops were due to re-embark for the return voyage to Cyprus.

On Sunday evening the ships sailed to join the Malta convoy 100 miles south of Cyprus, making contact with it on Monday morning. That afternoon, the combined convoy joined up with the French and the entire armada moved in towards the Egyptian coast. It was a magnificent sight, and the men's morale was high. The nine o'clock news on Sunday evening had been followed by a message from Anthony Eden, and it was heartening stuff. No one took much notice when, on Monday evening, the Leader of the Opposition spoke of a disastrous policy, and of a Prime Minister utterly discredited in the eyes of the world.

CHAPTER NINE

THE AIR ATTACKS

In accordance with Phase One of the *Musketeer* plan, the object of which was the elimination of the Egyptian Air Force before it could interfere with the Allied convoys sailing towards their objectives along the Egyptian coast or with the air drops, the bombing of the Egyptian airfields was scheduled to begin at 16.15 GMT on 31 October. Before that, while daylight lasted, eleven reconnaissance sorties were flown over the target areas, four by Canberras and seven by RF-84Fs. The French PR results, thanks to the fact that the *33eme Escadre* had the necessary processing and interpretation facilities based alongside it, were available very quickly, usually within an hour and a half; No 13 Squadron's films, on the other hand, had to be sent to Episkopi for processing, which could result in a delay of anything up to seven hours before the photographs were to hand. Nevertheless, the overall PR coverage was excellent, and was to remain so throughout the campaign, although not all the results reached the right people. As Paul Mallorie of 139 Squadron remembered[10]:

> Intelligence was very sparse . . . when we came to study our targets what we had to look at were old pages torn out of pilots' handbooks from the time the British were there. We did not see, in the whole of the operation, a single current photograph of the airfields and defences that we were going against, although we did see photographs of our raid results afterwards.

Some photographs of relevance were also provided by the US Central Intelligence Agency, operating the high-altitude Lockheed U2 reconnaissance aircraft on surveillance missions over the Middle East, but the importance of these has been exaggerated; it was the Canberras and RF-84Fs that brought back the photographic intelligence of real value. The important point about the exchange of information between the Americans and the Anglo-French command was that it continued throughout the operation, despite the severe differences at senior political level.

When Air Marshal Barnett launched his Canberras and Valiants against the airfields on 31 October, the marker Canberras from Cyprus actually took off after the main force had left, as the B.6s were going in at low level and therefore did not have to climb to altitude and form up. The plan called for the Valiants from Malta, which were equipped with a combined Navigation and Bombing System (NBS) – only recently fitted and as yet not very reliable – to drop proximity markers that would guide the marker force to its targets.

Things went wrong from the beginning. As No 139 Squadron's Canberras were about to leave their dispersals, the crew of the aircraft piloted by Flt Lt John Slater, whose target was Cairo West, were startled to hear a banging on the fuselage door. It transpired that, earlier in the day, Anthony Eden had been approached by the US Ambassador in London, who was concerned for the safety of US citizens being evacuated from Cairo to Alexandria by a road that passed very close to Cairo West. In fact, the road had been rebuilt and re-routed and was now a good ten miles clear of the airfield, but nobody realised this; the maps that had been consulted were out of date. The result, in Whitehall, was something close to panic, and a most urgent signal was sent to General Keightley in Cyprus instructing him to cancel the Cairo West attack.

Unfortunately, it was not sent to the commander of the Air Task Force, who was controlling the operation; by the time it filtered through, the Malta force was already on its way and the Cyprus Canberras were just getting airborne. The then Group Captain Lewis Hodges, who was Station Commander at Marham and who had gone out to Malta with the Valiant Wing, recalls that[11]

We never received any instructions at all through the normal command chain from Cyprus, but I received a personal signal direct from the Chief of the Air Staff, Sir Dermot Boyle, saying that on no account was Cairo West airfield to be bombed that night. The first wave of Valiants was on its way to Cairo; this created enormous problems, because of course there were four or five subsequent waves due to take off immediately afterwards. I initiated an immediate recall of the first wave on WT, but in addition the routeing of the aircraft was very near to El Adem and we were in communication with El Adem to give a verbal instruction by RT in plain language to recall these aircraft to Luqa. This was successful and the aircraft were recalled, but we had a situation where eight Valiants were returning to Luqa with full bomb loads and further waves were taking off to go to Cairo. We had to have the bombs jettisoned and you can imagine the problems of landing these aircraft, with others taking off, on a single runway. It was a very difficult operation and the air traffic control at Luqa, which was RAF but working with the Malta Civil Aviation Authority, did a marvellous job.

The target was hurriedly switched to Almaza, for which Flt Lt Slater and his crew now headed. The Canberras of the main force destined for Cairo West were also switched to Almaza, and by the time the signal reached them they were only ten minutes away from the target area, which gave their navigators a great deal of work to do in very little time. The outcome was that, although Almaza was successfully marked and there was good air-to-air communication between the marker aircraft and the main force, the latter erroneously bombed Cairo International Airport, which was adjacent to Almaza. The latter airfield was attacked in a second raid some three hours later, and considerable damage was caused.

Canberras and Valiants also attacked Kabrit, Abu Sueir and Inchas on this first night of operations. Although keeping a constant lookout for MiG-15s and Meteor night-fighters proved a great distraction to the crews (and contributed to the confusion that resulted in the bombing of Cairo International), the anticipated reaction from the enemy defences failed to materialise. In fact, Cairo and every town in the Nile Delta was ablaze with light; only after the first bombs fell did the Egyptians impose a blackout. The sighting of a solitary Meteor NF.13 was reported by the crew of a No 148 Squadron Valiant, but the Egyptian aircraft was well below the bomber's 40,000-foot altitude and made no attempt to attack.

At first light on 1 November, the land-based and carrier-borne strike squadrons took over the task of eliminating the Egyptian Air Force. Targets to the west of the 32° line of longitude were attacked by the Royal Navy's fighter-bombers, while those to the east were hit by the RAF ground attack aircraft from Cyprus, the French Thunderstreaks being assigned to the top cover role.

An hour before daybreak, as the last of the night's high-level bombers were returning to their bases, the Venom FB.4s of Nos 6, 8 and 249 Squadrons, together with the F-84Fs of the *3eme Escadre*, took off from Cyprus on their first mission of the day. At the same time, fifty miles off the Egyptian coast, the aircraft carriers *Albion, Bulwark* and *Eagle* had turned into wind and were preparing to launch their aircraft, having held their Wyverns, Sea Hawks and Sea Venoms at readiness for some hours. The two French light carriers, the *Arromanches* and *Lafayette*, with their complements of piston-engined Corsairs and Skyraiders, would cover the air- and seaborne landings later on, once the Egyptian Air Force had been destroyed; in the meantime, their task was to seek out and disable Egyptian warships that might pose a threat to the inbound convoys.

The Venoms' flight plan was to climb to 35,000 feet immediately after take-off and maintain this altitude until twenty miles from the target, when they would descend to make their attacks. Depending on the distance of the target from Cyprus, this allowed ten to fifteen minutes at low level over the target at full throttle, after which the return flight was to be made at 30-40,000 feet. Burdened as they were with rockets and external fuel tanks, the Venoms and the Naval strike aircraft were in no position to challenge any MiGs that might appear, hence the assignment of the F-84Fs to the fighter role.

The Operations Record Book of No 6 Squadron describes its own part in the day's events.

> From dawn throughout the day the Venom Wing here at Akrotiri
> was operating against the Egyptian airfields adjacent to the Suez

Canal. The first Venom aircraft to strike Egypt were a section of eight led by Squadron Leader Ellis, our Squadron Commander. Taking off at 05.15 hours, they were on target at 'S' hour which was 06.04 hours local time. Attacking Kasfareet and Kabrit they encountered no enemy aircraft in the air, and the only opposition was meagre and inaccurate anti-aircraft fire. Two MiG-15s were destroyed and an unidentified piston-engined aircraft damaged.

Heartened by the reports of the first section, the subsequent missions took off in high spirits, morale being very high throughout the squadron. In all, 34 sorties were flown today, including one by Group Captain MacDonald, the Station Commander. Thirteen Egyptian aircraft were destroyed and fifteen damaged. The airfields attacked were Kasfareet, Abu Sueir, Fayid and Shallufah. Three hangars were destroyed and four left burning, further ones being sprayed with cannon fire. Buildings, fuel bowsers and soft-skinned vehicles were also attacked. A large number of MiG-15s were found at Abu Sueir when the first section, led by Flight Lieutenant Harrison, arrived there on the second wave. Indeed seven of them were destroyed by our four Venoms and a further two were damaged. There were still many left dispersed around the airfield when the section left . . . Throughout the operations the aircraft continued to carry 600 rounds of semi-armour-piercing incendiary and high explosive incendiary ammunition. In addition today all aircraft carried four semi-armour-piercing high explosive rocket projectiles. Four of our Venoms were slightly damaged in today's operations.

The first Naval strikes of the day were carried out by 40 aircraft from the three British carriers, which launched their squadrons at 03.30 GMT to attack Cairo West, Almaza and Inchas. One high priority target was assigned to a strike of Sea Hawks; this was an Egyptian tank landing ship, the *Akka*, which had been located in Lake Timsah. Indications were that it was about to be used to block the Canal. The attack was duly made and the pilots left the area under the impression that their target was sinking. In fact it was not, and the ship was towed into the Canal and sunk across the fairway, which remained blocked for several months.

The airfield attacks by the Naval aircraft, meanwhile, had gone well. At Cairo West, Sea Hawk pilots from *Bulwark* found some

Il-28s and left them in flames. Only light AA fire was encountered, and all the aircraft returned safely to their carriers. Later in the day, when the carriers had established a steady rhythm, turning into wind and flying off strikes every 65 minutes, attacks were extended to the airfields at Bilbeis, Helwan and Heliopolis and to the coastal airfield of Dekhelia, near Alexandria, which was dive-bombed by Westland Wyverns from HMS *Eagle*.

The first day of November saw naval action, too, first of all in the Gulf of Suez, where the British cruiser HMS *Newfoundland* was on station. She was engaged, bravely if somewhat rashly, by the Egyptian frigate *Domiat*; the cruiser opened up with her main armament, and after a brief exchange of fire the Egyptian warship capsized and sank. A little later, in the Mediterranean, Corsairs from the *Arromanches* made rocket attacks on a Skoryii class destroyer, which they set on fire.

Between dawn and dusk on this first full day of operations the Royal Navy flew 205 strike sorties and the RAF 106; the French F-84Fs added seventy-five to this total. At the end of the day, Allied intelligence became aware that very few of Nassers's Il-28 jet bombers had been destroyed or damaged; air reconnaissance revealed that most of them had been evacuated to Luxor, situated about 270 miles up the Nile valley south of Cairo. This was beyond the range of the ground attack aircraft, but it could still be reached by the Valiants and Canberras and, as the Il-28s still posed a substantial threat to the Cyprus base, Luxor was placed on the target list for the night of 1/2 November.

Both bomber Wings were fully employed in the airfield attacks that night. Twenty-four Canberras and Valiants attacked Cairo West, eighteen Canberras and Valiants went to Fayid, sixteen Canberras and Valiants to Kasfareet and twenty-four Canberras to Luxor. In all, they dropped 429 1,000 lb bombs on the four airfields.

Crews returning from Luxor reported that the airfield had been badly hit, but post-strike reconnaissance by a 13 Squadron Canberra at 12.40 GMT on 2 November told a different tale. No bombs had fallen on the airfield, and the Il-28s were all intact.

Phase Two of the air attack plan, which was to have been implemented on 2 November, had envisaged attacks on selected key point targets, some in urban areas, associated with a psychological warfare campaign designed to reduce the Egyptian will to resist. World opinion, however, coupled with a growing reluctance by the British Government to risk unnecessary civilian casualties, resulted in a last-minute change, and General Keightley issued instructions that only military targets were to be attacked during this phase. The one exception was Cairo Radio, which was located in the Cairo suburb of Abu Zabac; it was believed that its destruction would have a serious effect on Egyptian morale.

At 08.00, twenty Canberras of the Cyprus Wing, escorted by twelve F-84Fs, took off to attack the radio station; it was the first time during the campaign that the Canberras had operated in broad daylight. The raid turned out to be something of a fiasco because the Canberra crews were briefed to bomb from between 3,000 and 4,000 feet, at a speed of 350 knots, and at that combination of height and speed the target was not visible in their bombsights. Moreover, the attack involved a rapid letdown from high altitude, which meant that the observers had to change to low level map reading, and this proved to be extremely difficult. To complicate matters still further, the marker flares dropped by 139 Squadron were partly hidden by trees and were not seen until it was too late to attack accurately. The upshot was that the bombs either overshot or undershot the target, causing only superficial damage, and Cairo Radio was back on the air again after only a brief period of silence.

In contrast, attacks on military targets that day were generally successful. RAF Venoms flew 100 sorties in the course of the day and the Huckstep Camp, where reconnaissance had revealed a large concentration of tanks and other military vehicles, was heavily attacked. In one strike on this target by seven Venoms of No 6 Squadron, each aircraft carrying eight squash head rockets, several tanks were destroyed or damaged, a small building in the tank compound exploded and many soft-skinned vehicles were disabled by cannon fire. The attacks were pressed home through considerable AA fire at very low level without loss, although one pilot returned to Cyprus with part of a lorry axle embedded in a wing tank. Huckstep was again attacked that evening by 19 Canberras and 5 Valiants, which dropped 128 bombs.

The crews of the Royal Navy's strike aircraft had a busy

74

day, flying 189 sorties. The pilots averaged four sorties a day, alternating their strike missions with periods of combat air patrol. Every 20 minutes, the carriers of the Naval Task Force, steaming at 30 knots in a fixed pattern, turned their bows into wind to enable aircraft to be launched or landed while the hours of daylight lasted. On one sortie, a Sea Venom of No 893 Squadron, flown by Lieutenant-Commander Wilcox, was badly hit by ground fire and the observer – Flying Officer R.C. Olding, RAF – was seriously injured. Olding continued to assist his pilot as the latter flew back to make a successful wheels-up landing on the deck of HMS *Eagle*, but his left leg had to be amputated. He was awarded the Distinguished Service Cross.

Meanwhile, the air defence squadrons on Cyprus remained on full alert throughout the Allied air attacks in case of retaliatory raids by Egyptian jet bombers. The Allied commanders had a good indication of what was likely to happen in that event when a practice air-raid drill was laid on in Famagusta; it resulted in a panic-stricken riot in the docks area, and troops trying to close the dock gates as part of the exercise were almost trampled to death by a frantic horde of dock workers, fleeing for their lives.

By nightfall on 2 November, the Egyptian Air Force had been virtually eliminated as a fighting force. Intelligence gleaned from reconnaissance photographs indicated that the air attacks had destroyed 91 out of 110 MiG-15s, or 83 per cent: eleven out of fourteen Meteors (85 per cent); and 30 out of 44 Vampires (70 per cent).

There remained the Il-28s. On 31 October forty-eight of these aircraft had been identified; of these, six had so far been destroyed in air attacks and twenty-one had been flown south to Luxor. That left another twenty-one, of which a small number were known to be at Cairo International, still out of bounds to air attack, but the rest seemed to have disappeared, along with a number of MiGs. They had, in fact, been flown to Riyadh in Saudi Arabia, where they refuelled before flying on to Syria. The MiGs stayed there, but the Il-28s were returned to the Soviet Union for the time being.

Luxor was again attacked at last light on 2 November. The markers came from No 139 Squadron, which on this occasion carried a mixed load of target indicators and 1,000 lb bombs.

Having dive-bombed with TIs, the markers were briefed to see the raid through and then add their own contribution of straight and level attacks with the thousand-pounders. 'By then,' Air Vice-Marshal Paul Mallorie recalls[12], 'the gyros were completely toppled, the navigators confused and the bomb sights useless. So we made dive-bombing attacks on the parked Beagle aircraft which were there, with high explosives.' On this occasion the attack enjoyed some success, three Il-28s being destroyed; but again, most of the bombs fell wide of the airfield.

Concerns about an apparent build-up of Soviet-built combat aircraft in Syria resulted in part of No 13 Squadron's photo-reconnaissance effort being diverted in that direction. Allied intelligence also knew of a plan, fostered by Egypt, called Operation *Beisan*, which envisaged an offensive by Syrian and Jordanian forces aimed at cutting Israel in two and reaching the Mediterranean at Nathanya. The PR operations over Syria resulted in the RAF's only Canberra loss of the campaign, when PR.7 WH799 was intercepted by a Syrian Air Force Meteor NF.13 and shot down on 6 November. The navigator, Fg Off Urquhart-Pullen, was killed; the pilot, Flt Lt B.L. Hunter, and a third crew member were injured and detained in Beirut Military Hospital. They were later repatriated.

With the Egyptian Air Force rendered ineffective, the Allied air forces switched their emphasis to armed reconnaissances of roads and railways leading from Ismailia to Cairo and to the Great Bitter Lake, the jet aircraft now being joined by the French Navy's Corsairs. During one of the first attacks of the morning a small force of Canberras, escorted by Hunters, bombed the Almaza barracks. The raid was not particularly important, except for one unexpected result: although only 30 per cent of the bombs fell in the barracks area, ten out of thirteen MiG-15s parked on a road between the barracks and Almaza airfield were destroyed or damaged. Later, the Canberra crews discovered that British and French naval aircraft had been operating beneath them, their pilots unaware of the raid taking place at a higher level.

The Hunters again provided an escort when, an hour later, twenty-two Canberras dropped 126 bombs on the important Nfisha marshalling yards near Ismailia, the target being marked by two Canberras of No 18 Squadron. The Canberras attacked in a shallow dive and thirty-six of their bombs exploded in the main yards, others hitting the railway tracks leading into the marshalling area as well as setting fire to a fuel storage area and an oil tank. The attack, which was designed to hamper the movement of Egyptian forces towards Port Said, blocked all through lines and sidings.

Another high-priority target, Gamil Bridge – which carried the only road connecting Port Said to the Nile Delta – was assigned to the Royal Navy. It was dive-bombed by Sea Hawks and Wyverns from HMS *Eagle*'s air group, but it was a concrete structure with eleven supporting columns and their bombs only succeeded in chipping large chunks off the columns. During this attack a Wyvern flown by Lieutenant D.F. MacCarthy was hit by AA fire; he limped out to sea, his aircraft smoking badly, and ejected. Although he had come down only 4,000 yards from a shore battery, aircraft from *Eagle* and *Bulwark* maintained a defensive CAP overhead until a rescue helicopter arrived from *Eagle*, some seventy miles away. He was returned on board after two hours, unhurt.

In a second attack on the bridge the Navy pilots changed their tactics, the Sea Hawks attacking at low level armed with 500 lb bombs with 30-second delay fuses. These penetrated the bridge and its supports like darts; the destructive effect of the explosions was enhanced by the confined spaces in which the bombs had lodged, and the bridge collapsed.

HMS *Albion* withdrew to refuel on 3 November in readiness to support the impending sea and airborne landings, but the other two carriers kept up a steady cycle of attacks. Egyptian forces, many of them withdrawn from Sinai, were flooding into the Cairo area, and the weight of the Allied fighter-bomber offensive continued to be directed against lines of communication. The roads running from the west towards Port Said soon became blocked with burnt-out transport and armoured fighting vehicles. The task of the fighter-bomber pilots was now complicated as the roads had become choked with refugees, streaming away from the Canal Zone, and great care had to be exercised to avoid attacking civilians by mistake.

The Royal Navy's fighter-bombers caused great damage to the Huckstep Barracks in a series of attacks during the day.

French Corsairs dive-bombed Almaza and Dekhelia, one of their squadron commanders being shot down. French F-84Fs made a rocket attack on a radar station at Abu Sultan and wiped it out; they also lost an aircraft, with its pilot killed.

Pilots returning from air strikes reported that the accuracy of the enemy anti-aircraft fire had now improved considerably, no doubt as the Egyptian gunners got used to coping with aircraft speeds of 400 mph or more over the target. Since this growing efficiency posed a serious threat to the slow-flying transport aircraft, which were to carry out the airdrop on the following Monday (it was now Saturday), the strike aircraft were detailed to silence as many anti-aircraft batteries as possible, especially around Port Said. It was a difficult and dangerous task, and many of the aircraft returned to their carriers or airfields with varying degrees of battle damage.

Neither of the two British fatalities suffered on 3 November, however, was attributable to enemy action. In the first incident, a Sea Hawk went over the side while landing on HMS *Bulwark*, killing the pilot, Sub-Lieutenant C.J. Hall; and the second occurred when a Venom of No 8 Squadron hit the ground. This happened when a formation of four aircraft, having completed an armed reconnaissance between El Kantara and Ismailia, set off to make a planned strike on Abu Sueir. As they skimmed the sand dunes at 30 feet, the number four in the formation suddenly saw the number three aircraft, about 100 yards ahead, cartwheeling across the ground, shedding fragments as it went. The pilot, Flt Lt E.A. Sheehan, was killed.

No 6 Squadron's ORB report typifies the day's work carried out by the RAF ground attack squadrons:

> Today our missions were switched from strikes on airfield targets to armed reconnaissance in specified areas. There were four missions in all, each of four aircraft. In spite of this easing up of effort compared to the previous two days, targets were becoming increasingly hard to find. There was no opposition from anti-aircraft fire throughout the day, and none of our aircraft were damaged. The first section claimed the only MiG-15 destroyed, and the second section found two Meteor 8s apparently ready to fly at Fayid. These and an oil bowser were left burning; the

section also claimed two Sherman-based armoured personnel carriers destroyed. Our next section which visited Fayid also, observed a staff car drawn up by the Meteor 8s destroyed by our previous mission. The occupants were contemplating the still smouldering wreckage, and as they ran for cover the staff car erupted behind them. Attention was focussed on it since it represented the only undamaged machinery in sight.

The RAF flew 53 ground attack sorties on 3 November, and the Royal Navy 131. The French Navy, now that its Corsairs were cleared for action, contributed many more, as did the French F-84Fs. On Sunday 4 November, with the invasion fleet approaching Egypt, HMS *Eagle* withdrew for replenishment and to receive replacement aircraft from El Adem. *Eagle*'s crew made use of the break to repair the carrier's starboard catapult, which had been out of action during the whole operation. She returned to station that night, fully serviceable. HMS *Albion* was also back on station by now, so that the support carrier force was up to full strength.

The primary targets now, in the hours before invasion, were the Egyptian coastal defences, with emphasis on objectives in the Port Said area. For example, Sqn Ldr Maitland, OC 249 Squadron, led two formations of four Venoms on a successful strike against anti-aircraft guns at Port Said, while No 6 Squadron destroyed a MiG-15 at Abu Sueir and a Vampire T.11 at Fayid. Both squadrons then attacked their secondary targets, radar and anti-aircraft installations around Gamil airport, attacking through light and inaccurate flak and causing much damage.

At 16.45 GMT, seven Valiants and nine Canberras from Malta and four Canberras from Cyprus attacked the radar and coastal gun emplacements on El Agami island. Anti-aircraft fire was heavy - probably the heaviest encountered in the whole campaign - but no aircraft were damaged. An hour later, six Valiants and twelve Canberras from Malta, backed up by four marker Canberras from Cyprus, pounded Huckstep Barracks, this time with little opposition.

Shortly before nightfall, Sea Hawks from HMS *Bulwark* made a successful attack with rockets and cannon on four Egyptian motor torpedo boats, which had been reported by air reconnaissance to be heading out of Alexandria in the direction of the Naval Task Force. One boat blew up, two more were set on fire and the fourth was damaged but still able to pick up survivors.

Credit for the most successful attack of the day, however, belonged to the *Armée de l'Air*. Air Chief Marshal Sir Denis Smallwood, then Group Captain (Plans) with the Air Task Force, recollects that 'We were in the Ops Room, considering how best to destroy the Il-28s at Luxor, when General Brohan looked in and offered his help. He disappeared, and returned a few hours later to say that it had been done, and produced photographs to prove it!'[13]

The mission was carried out by the F-84Fs of Colonel Maurice Perdrizet's *1ere Escadre* from Lydda. Fitted with long range fuel tanks, they crossed Sinai and the Gulf of Suez and attacked Luxor in two waves, one of eight aircraft and one of twelve, using cannon only. Post-strike reconnaissance by an RF-84F, backed up by a Canberra sortie, confirmed that all 18 Il-28s at Luxor had been destroyed.

As night fell over Cyprus, ground crews continued working on the Hastings, Valetta and Noratlas transport aircraft to get them on top line for the coming operation, while men of the 16th Parachute Brigade Group and their French counterparts made final studies of target maps and photographs. On the carriers and the Cyprus airfields, the fighter-bomber pilots snatched a few hours' sleep. Their first task had been successfully accomplished, but with the coming of morning they would be committed at maximum strength to provide close support for the Allied forces as Phase Three of the operation got underway.

Under cover of darkness, a lone Handley Page Hastings transport aircraft dropped half a million leaflets over Cairo, urging the Egyptian Government to accept the Allied ultimatum. No attempt was made to intercept it; there was no longer an Egyptian Air Force to challenge it.

CHAPTER TEN

THE AIRBORNE ASSAULT

The airborne unit selected to spearhead the British invasion task force was the 3rd Parachute Battalion, commanded by Colonel Paul Crook. Its objective was Gamil, the airfield on the outskirts of Port Said. The choice of a single battalion was dictated by the fact that the Cyprus airfields could not accommodate sufficient transport aircraft to carry a force of more than battalion strength, in this case 668 men and their equipment. The plan was for the remainder of the 16th Parachute Brigade to follow on either by air or sea once the objective had been secured.

It could hardly be said that the Brigade was experienced in this type of operation. The last time British paratroops had carried out a major drop under combat conditions had been in March 1945, during the Rhine crossing at Wesel. The standard of their weapons also left much to be desired; they carried normal British infantry equipment, which meant that most of their arms and ammunition had to be dropped separately in containers. Only the despised Sten gun (which was prone to jamming and often thankfully discarded in action when the paratroops seized better-class enemy weapons) was small and light enough to be carried during the drop, but even this practice had been vetoed for fear that the gun might become entangled in the parachute harness or interfere with the static line and cause an accident. This lack of small-arms support and the consequent inability to return any fire from the ground meant that the paratroops would be at the mercy of the defenders on the way down, a state of affairs that filled many with misgivings, although morale remained generally good. Even when the men were on the ground, there would be a further delay while they broke open their weapons containers, and cover on the airfield was likely to be sparse. It was clear that a great deal was going to depend on the supporting Allied strike aircraft.

The men were to be lifted into action by two types of RAF transport aircraft: the four-engined Handley Page Hastings and the twin-engined Vickers Valetta. Neither was particularly suited to the task, having only a single side-exit door, but the planned re-equipment of RAF Transport Command, despite the fact that both the Army and the RAF had long advocated the establishment of a strong strategic airborne reserve and the provision of aircraft capable of ferrying it to any destination worldwide at a few hours' notice, had received lower priority than the re-equipment of the other operational Commands. In 1956, the emphasis was on nuclear strategy, with its associated building up of the V-Force, and on the modernisation of Fighter Command.

The fact that the Hastings and Valetta both had side-loading freight doors meant the type of equipment which could be transported and air-dropped in support of the paratroops was severely restricted. There was no possibility at all of dropping heavy guns and transport; even ammunition and supplies, which in the case of tail-loading aircraft like the French Noratlas could be rolled out of the rear doors on platforms and parachuted down in bulk, had to be packed into special containers that were slung under the fuselages of the British transports. The packaging of these supplies was a major operation in itself, involving countless man-hours and necessitating the fitting of special delivery equipment to the transport aircraft. The only vehicle capable of being dropped by the Hastings was an old wartime jeep, which was brought out of storage for the operation.

The French paratroop force, 492 men of the *2eme Regiment Parachutistes Coloniaux* (RPC) under Colonel Pierre Château-Jobert, who was known to all and sundry as 'Conan', were far better equipped and experienced. While the British paratroops carried out only one large-scale training drop per year, the French training programme included a drop at least once a month. Moreover, the French Paras had been in almost constant action since the end of World War II, either in Indo-China or Algeria, and they had refined their weapons and techniques as a result. They were equipped with specially designed rifles and sub-machine guns with folding butts, enabling them to be carried across the chest during the parachute descent, so that when a paratrooper landed he could go into action immediately.

The standard French transport aircraft was the Nord Noratlas, a twin-boom, twin-engined aircraft with tail loading doors. It could carry thirty-five fully equipped paratroops, compared with twenty each for the Hastings and Valetta, together with their personal equipment and support weapons, or alternatively platform loads of vehicles and artillery. The French, too, had an easy informality born of experience. Five minutes before a drop, when the red warning light came on inside the aircraft, the paratroops would carry out a swift but thorough check of each others' harness and equipment and then, on the signal of the green light, they would jump in two streams from both sides of the Noratlas's fuselage with one parachutist following right on the heels of the man in front. This meant that a complete stick of seventeen paras could exit from the aircraft in ten seconds, which in turn meant that under favourable conditions, the stick would be spread out over no more than half a mile. A typical stick of fifteen British paratroops, carried by the Hastings, took twenty seconds to leave the aircraft and was spread out over one mile.

The operational plan, drafted by General Andre Beaufre, the French task force commander, envisaged the dropping of the 2eme RPC on a very narrow dropping zone in the Interior Basin between Lake Manzala and the Canal to the south of Port Said at Raswa. On D+1 a second regiment was to be dropped on El Kantara, and on D+2 a third regiment on El Kantara or an objective further south. The British, meanwhile, would land 2,500 men of the Royal Marine Commandos. An emergency plan to capture Port Said rapidly in the event of the collapse of the Egyptian Army was also drawn up; this plan, known as *Omelette*, called for a British parachute drop on Gamil, together with a helicopter assault by Royal Marine Commandos on the approaches to the south of the town, and a French air drop on Port Fuad, possibly with naval gunfire support. The airborne spearhead could be reinforced by further French parachute drops, first on Gamil and the next day on El Kantara and possibly Ismailia, while the remainder of the British 16th Parachute Brigade was brought in by sea. Having secured their objectives, these forces would then advance on Port Said, which was expected to succumb quickly. In this way it was hoped that the Canal Zone could be occupied within 24 hours, before the Egyptians had time to recover and regroup sufficiently to offer serious resistance, and that the forces in position would be able to hold on until the arrival of the main convoys some days later.

Omelette was an emergency plan for occupation, rather than for assault; it could only be implemented in the event of the Egyptians offering no opposition, and by 2 November that possibility was looking increasingly unlikely. The Egyptian defences in Port Said were being strengthened by units that had not yet been committed to the fighting in Sinai, and by others that had escaped being cut off by the Israelis and re-crossed the Canal. In addition, there were known to be a number of Soviet-built tanks and SP guns in the Port Said area, an unfavourable situation to be faced by a relatively weak airborne force relying on fighter-bombers for its sole support. In particular, the possibility of strong enemy opposition rendered the plan to use a helicopter assault force impracticable, hence the decision to use paratroops only.

As far as the British drop was concerned, the geographical location of Gamil airfield – which was about a mile and a half long and half a mile wide, bounded to the north and south by the sea – meant that the transport aircraft could approach only from the north-west or south-east, and each direction had its disadvantages. Coming in from the north-west meant that the pilots would be flying into the glare of the rising sun, and an approach from the south-east would take the aircraft directly over Port Said's heaviest anti-aircraft defences. There was little doubt that the airfield itself would be defended, since photo-reconnaissance had already revealed hundreds of large oil drums scattered over the field, obviously placed there to hamper any landing. (In the event, these drums – which were filled with sand – were to prove a blessing for the paratroops, providing useful cover for the men as they unpacked their containers and prepared to go into action.)

The French dropping zone at Raswa was even more restricted, being only 150 yards across and bounded by the sea, roads, the Canal and lines of trees. Had it not been for the compact dropping techniques practised by the French, it would probably have been considered inadequate. To Pierre Château-Jobert's experienced men, however, it presented no problem. Their first objective was the twin bridges near the waterworks crossing the interior basin waterway, a vital link on the Port Said–Suez road. After these had been taken, the paras were to attack the Port Fuad area on the opposite side of the Canal facing Port Said.

The British assault on Gamil was to be led by the Valettas, with the Hastings bringing up the rear. Each aircraft carried about twenty men of 3 Para, and the Hastings also carried underslung panniers containing heavy equipment. The air armada was to approach the objective in two columns, the aircraft flying in pairs. These pairs were to form boxes of six with the first two aircraft at 600 feet and those behind stepped up at intervals of 100 feet and fifteen seconds. It was hoped that this arrangement would give adequate time for the paratroops dropping from the aircraft in front to get clear by the time the second stick went down. Each box of aircraft would be separated by an interval of one minute, about two miles in terms of distance. Since the target was expected to be heavily defended, speed was of the essence, and the plan envisaged the whole British force being on the ground in eight minutes. To enable the paratroops to go into action quickly, heavy support equipment such as anti-tank guns was to be dropped by Hastings Mk II aircraft immediately after the last sticks of paratroops had gone down.

The French tactics in the drop were somewhat similar to the British in that their Noratlas transports were to approach the DZ in pairs, but the whole formation was much tighter, with 60 yards between each aircraft in any one pair and the pairs separated by a gap of 120 yards. Moreover, because of the confined nature of the DZ, the French decided to jump from an unusually low altitude of 400 feet; it was estimated that in this way the drop could be completed in four minutes.

Whereas the French paratroops had been ready for action since August, their British counterparts had to work hard to complete preparations in time for the assault. They had exactly a week between 29 October, when 3rd Battalion was called away from anti-terrorist operations in the Troodos Mountains, and 5 November to get everything ready. Sunday 4 November was a particularly busy day; it began with a drumhead service in the hot sun on a dusty parade ground, and in the afternoon each stick of parachutists was driven to Nicosia where the Transport Air Task Force, commanded by Group Captain B.R. Macnamara DSO, had assembled eighteen Valettas and fourteen Hastings. The soldiers travelled in trucks bearing numbers that corresponded with chalk marks on the aircraft parked around the perimeter. On arriving at their assigned aircraft, the men unloaded their heavy personal equipment containers from the vehicles and laid them in neat lines on the ground, where they were thoroughly checked; next, they were ordered to collect their parachutes from inside the aircraft and to put them on to make sure that the fit was accurate and comfortable. The parachutes were then replaced in the aircraft and the containers stacked neatly in the aisles.

Much last-minute anxiety had been caused in the preceding days by delays in the arrival of vital equipment such as parachutes and roller conveyors, with which heavy loads were to be dropped, and it was not until late in the afternoon of 1 November that this equipment reached Cyprus. Matters were further complicated by the fact that there was no mobile parachute packing section on the island, so that all parachutes had to be packed in the United Kingdom and then flown in. It was an incredible oversight, in view of the Parachute Brigade's role as part of Britain's Strategic Reserve.

Some concern was also expressed by the transport pilots over the lack of sun visors, since they would be flying directly into the low-angle sun. One squadron of Valettas was in fact fitted with these devices, but the main transport force had been held in Britain until the last moment to reduce overcrowding on Cyprus and there was insufficient time to fit the visors to the bulk of the aircraft. As it turned out, the glare did not impair the success of the drop in any way, and even without the visors the pilots managed to place their parachutists accurately on the DZ. There was one plus point: approaching Gamil into the sun, rather than over the Port Said AA defences, meant that the crews had no need to wear hot, heavy, armoured flak vests, which would have increased their fatigue factor tremendously.

Despite all the fears and difficulties, the assault plan was as ready as it could be by nightfall on 4 November. And there was another fact that greatly relieved the Allied commanders: during the night, the US Sixth Fleet, which had been on station in the eastern Mediterranean to protect the evacuation of American nationals, withdrew from the operational area.

The first wave of Valettas began taking off from Nicosia at 03.00 GMT on 5 November and executed a night form-up before setting course for Egypt at 500 feet. Because of the densely populated and restricted nature of the assault areas, normal marking techniques involving the drop of a small number of 'pathfinder' parachutists close to the DZs with the task of marking the run-in to the zones with flares, and the point at which the paratroops were to be dropped by means of a cloth T, were out of the question. Four Canberras from Nos 18 and 139 Squadrons were therefore detailed to mark both DZs with 1,000 lb TIs, natural features being selected to mark the release points. In the case of Gamil airfield, the main natural feature was a sea wall, and the French had the beach immediately to the west of their zone. The marker aircraft left Nicosia after the transport force, overtook it and placed their markers accurately at Gamil before proceeding to mark the French DZ at the Interior Basin south of Port Said.

Escort for the transports was provided by the Hawker Hunters of Nos 1 and 34 Squadrons, whose pilots flew a protective sweep ahead and circled the DZ, alert for signs of opposition. The fighter leader was concerned that the transport serials would prove difficult to defend, strung out as they were over a number of miles, but his fears were unfounded; no enemy aircraft came up to challenge the incoming force. In the Port Fuad area, F-84Fs carried out a similar sweep ahead of the Noratlas transports from Tymbou, which had taken off shortly after the British force. Naval aircraft also provided top cover, the carrier squadrons providing up to eighteen aircraft per mission. These ranged far and wide over the Nile Delta and as far south as Cairo, but encountered no opposition.

As the transports flew on over the Mediterranean, a last-minute change in the dropping order had to be made. This was caused by the fact that the Hastings Mk Is, which had been the last to take off from Cyprus with their paratroop serials and which were to have overtaken the Hastings Mk IIs carrying the loads of heavy equipment en route, were subjected to more than the expected amount of drag from their under-fuselage equipment containers and made far slower progress than had been anticipated. This meant that over the objective, some of the heavy equipment would have to be dropped before the paratroops had all gone down. Fortunately, this change in the proceedings did not compromise the operation in any way.

Armed reconnaissance and ground attack missions on and around the two DZs were carried out respectively by the Venoms and Thunderstreaks from Akrotiri and the naval aircraft. These cleared the area as the British airborne force approached Gamil at 05.15 GMT, led by the Valettas of No 114 Squadron under Sqn Ldr D.B. Delaney AFC. It was a bright and colourful morning, with good visibility, and one officer of 3 Para later wrote of being impressed by the 'Turquoise sky, buff sand, slate sea and black smoke in a great pall towering out of the control tower buildings.'

With a minute to go, the paratroops came to action stations and moved to their jumping positions. Then the green lights went on and the first sticks launched themselves into space. Within ten minutes 85 per cent of the British force was on the ground. Four paratroops came to grief during the drop: two men drifted out to sea and almost drowned before they were able to struggle free of their equipment and swim ashore, a third landed in a minefield and was killed, and the fourth came down on the top of the control tower and was seriously injured.

There was nothing like the anticipated volume of enemy fire, although a dozen paratroops were wounded by small-arms and mortars. Heavy equipment also landed on target, although some pilots had to make two runs to get their loads away safely. The volume of Egyptian anti-aircraft fire was moderate, although inaccurate. Nine aircraft were damaged, but all regained Cyprus safely. One Hastings pilot, Flt Lt J.A. King DSO DFC, suffered engine trouble that caused him to fall behind the main stream. His aircraft was heavily laden with fourteen paratroops, a jeep and trailer and six containers and he could maintain a speed that was only three knots above the safety margin, but by skilfully shutting down and restarting his overheating engines in sequence he reached the DZ and dropped his load accurately. He was awarded the AFC.

Vickers Valiants pictured at RAF Luqa, Malta, during the Suez operation.

Israeli Air Force Dassault Ouragan fighter-bomber.

The three fighter-bomber types used by the Royal Navy's strike squadrons in 'Musketeer': the Hawker Sea Hawk (*above*), de Havilland Sea Venom (*below*) and Westland Wyvern (*facing top*).

The Bristol Sycamore, which could carry three soldiers, was one of the types used by the Joint Experimental Helicopter Unit, the other being the Westland Whirlwind.

North American F-51 Mustangs of the Israeli Air Force. These aircraft played a key role in the defeat of the Egyptian forces in Sinai.

Israeli Air Force Gloster Meteor F.8. One of these aircraft shot down an Il-14 carrying eighteen members of the Egyptian General Staff on 29 October 1956.

Centurion tanks of 6 RTR move up in support of British troops in Port Said.

A British patrol bringing up rations passes a burnt-out car in Port Said.

Egyptian civilians scavenging in the rubble of Port Said a week after the ceasefire.

French minesweeper passes a confiscated Egyptian fishing boat, flying the White Ensign, on the Suez Canal late in November.

Soldiers inspecting a Russian-made SU-100 self-propelled gun, knocked out by Allied fighter-bombers.

A Naval diver goes down to start work on salvage operations, clearing sunken blockships from the Suez Canal.

British troops supervise the collection of captured Egyptian small-arms. The older weapons were destroyed, the more modern Soviet equipment retained for evaluation.

Scottish troops enjoy a game of cards in their desert outpost while waiting to be relieved by members of the UN peacekeeping force.

As the transport aircraft turned back towards Cyprus to pick up reinforcements and supplies, 3 Para rapidly got organised. It was split into three companies, each of which had been assigned a specific task. A Company, which had dropped closest to the release point, had the task of securing the north-west corner of the airfield. B Company, which had dropped last in order to land on the Port Said end of the airfield, was responsible for sealing off that area. The third Company, which comprised Battalion HQ, Brigade HQ and the various supporting units had dropped in the middle, could be diverted to wherever its assistance was most needed.

A and B Companies quickly went into action. They had no trouble in occupying the control tower, which was still burning from the air attacks. A Company then began to move out towards the north-west, mopping up Egyptian positions as they advanced. The strongest opposition came from an enemy pillbox, but this was put out of action by the first round from a rocket launcher that went through the firing slit, killing two of the defenders and wounding the remaining eight, who surrendered. B Company at the Port Said end of the airfield had a stiffer fight on its hands, having landed right on top of the Egyptian defences. One paratrooper, for example, watched an Egyptian shooting straight at him from below as he neared the ground; the enemy soldier had climbed out of his slit trench to get a better view. A late oscillation of the British soldier's parachute swung his container, which was dangling below him, like a giant pendulum and it knocked the Egyptian sprawling into his foxhole. There was a brief and bloody hand-to-hand encounter before the defenders were overwhelmed and the paratroops were able to move on to their next objective.

Meanwhile, the Battalion's mortar platoon in the centre of the field was dropping a rapid succession of rounds on enemy positions in the sewage farm a mile away to the south-east. One group of paratroops was pinned down by accurate fire from an Egyptian anti-tank gun, firing from the beach, but this was soon knocked out by a 106 mm recoilless rifle shell. Because some of the radio equipment had been damaged in the drop, there was some delay in establishing contact with the Fleet Air Arm fighter-bombers; nevertheless, the paratroops were never without constant air cover. In fact, there were never sufficient targets available for the pilots to engage, and many of them sought targets of opportunity in the surrounding area rather than return to their carriers with their aircraft still armed.

The naval pilots operating in direct support of the 3 Para landing were briefed by R/T from the ground, using a co-ordinated fire plan. They worked over their allotted targets, some of which were only one or two hundred yards ahead of the troops, for exactly nine and a half minutes before withdrawing to allow the advance to continue. Wyverns from HMS *Eagle*, meanwhile, attacked the Coastguard Barracks on the western side of Port Said; the strike leader, Lt-Cdr Cowling, scored a direct hit with his 1,000 lb delayed action bomb, but his aircraft was hit and he had to use his ejection seat about ten miles out to sea. He was picked up by rescue helicopter and returned safely to his ship.

Within forty-five minutes, the paratroops had succeeded in overcoming all resistance on Gamil airfield. By noon, the runways had been cleared sufficiently to accept the arrival of Allied transport aircraft. But Gamil had been built to operate Dakotas and its runways were not long enough for the Hastings and Valettas, so the remainder of 3 Para was dropped that afternoon by five aircraft.

With Gamil secured, Whirlwind helicopters from the aircraft carriers *Ocean* and *Theseus* began flying in stores, mainly medical supplies, and a regular shuttle service was quickly established. The helicopters brought in a doctor, chocolate, cigarettes, and 1,000 gallons of water stored in Bofors ammunition boxes. They also evacuated thirty-seven wounded men, including some French paratroops.

Fifteen minutes after the British assault on Gamil, the French Noratlas transports dropped Château-Jobert's 2eme RCP on the French DZ at Raswa. On landing, the French infantry came under heavy fire from Egyptian infantry concealed in slit trenches, and also from machine-guns sited near the bridge and Bofors anti-aircraft guns, which were able to rake the whole area. Fortunately, the DZ was heavily pitted with holes and craters in which the paratroops were able to take cover. General Jean Marcellin Gilles, commander of the French Airborne Task Force, flew over the area in a Noratlas that had been converted into a flying command post (an idea first used by the French in Indo-China and one which was now to prove invaluable) and saw that the paratroops were meeting with serious resistance. He quickly called in a strike of Avengers from the carrier *Lafayette* and Thunderstreaks from Cyprus, which were soon pounding the Egyptian defences. Gilles continued to circle the area throughout the whole battle, braving anti-aircraft fire that was often heavy, directing the movement of troops on the ground and the activities of the fighter-bombers as well as passing back a minute-by-minute report on the progress of the fighting to General Beaufre, who was at sea in the cruiser *Gustave Zede*, and to the Expeditionary Force HQ in Cyprus. An extraordinary personality, with one eye glaring out of a battered face, Gilles cared nothing for soldiers who did not wear the red beret. The British Military Attaché in Paris had once described him as 'the rudest, most unpleasant and most hostile French officer we have ever met'. But he produced results, and as a fighting soldier his reputation was second to none.

Once the enemy resistance had been overcome after some brisk hand-to-hand fighting, the French quickly reorganised and, reinforced by a second lift of men, moved towards their objective. The eastern road bridge across the interior basin had been destroyed but the western bridge was the objective of No 1 Company, which during the advance was heavily shelled by Egyptian tanks sited on the golf course behind the bridge. With characteristic dash, the French charged through the fire supported by their fighter-bombers and by 09.00 the bridge was in their hands.

The capture of the bridge, accomplished at a cost of ten French casualties, meant that the breakout from Port Said was now assured. The French were in control of the surrounding area and Château-Jobert set up his HQ in one of the waterworks buildings. The waterworks itself was undamaged, for which the French were thankful. In the event of the waterworks being destroyed, there had been a plan to ship in fresh water by sea and impose strict rationing on the civilian population, which would have caused enormous administrative problems. At 13.00, word reached the French that 3 Para had cleared the Gamil area and were pushing eastwards. The first phase of the assault was over.

CHAPTER ELEVEN

THE ADVANCE ON PORT SAID

Brigadier-General Salaheddin Moguy, the Egyptian Army's Chief of Staff, Eastern Command – who, as the senior officer present in the area, was to be in charge of the defence of Port Said – was under no illusion about the effectiveness of his assets. Although troops were continually re-crossing the Canal and entering the district, many were without arms or equipment. Yet morale was relatively high among the troops both at Port Said and Ismailia, and their company-strength resistance at the airfield itself and on the approach road to Port Said presented Colonel Crook's airborne battalion with no easy task. After clearing the airfield area the men had to negotiate ditches and fight their way through the thick reeds and swampy ground on the edge of the sewage farm, finally advancing through the cemetery and Port Said's slum suburbs before reaching the more modern built-up area.

The airfield's geographic location, with the sea on one side and the lake on the other, meant that the paratroops were unable to carry out any outflanking manoeuvres; instead, they had to advance straight along the road. After clearing the few huts and bungalows along the beach, they advanced up the narrow strip of sand to the line of tall reeds that marked the fringe of the sewage farm. It was here that they ran into the first really severe opposition; as they approached the reeds, they encountered heavy rifle and machine-gun fire from Egyptian troops positioned along the edge of the farm. Beyond the farm itself, SU-100 self-propelled guns opened up with a heavy barrage of shellfire, while from the dock area multiple rocket launchers also joined in. The latter were quickly silenced by the Fleet Air Arm's Sea Hawks and Wyverns, which also knocked out two of the SU-100s.

The task of clearing the thick, head-high reeds took the best part of an hour. Many Egyptian prisoners were taken and an SU-100, which had been lying hull down among the greenery and causing the paratroops a great deal of concern, was knocked out by a 106 mm recoilless anti-tank rifle. Even when they at last broke out on to the open terrain of the sewage farm, the paratroops' problems were still not over. As they advanced on the right of the farm the men came under heavy fire from the cemetery, with enemy machine-guns raking an exposed stretch of ground 400 yards across. There was another nasty moment when the paratroops, advancing across this exposed area, were strafed by a French Corsair, whose pilot mistook them for Egyptian forces. Fortunately, no casualties were sustained.

On the edge of the sewage farm the paratroops regrouped and made plans for the assault on the cemetery, while Allied air strikes on the Egyptian positions continued almost without pause. The paras quickly located the main enemy observation post from which most of the machine-gun fire was being directed; this was sited in a tall block of flats behind the sewage farm, and heavy small-arms fire was also coming from the Coastguard barrracks on the other side of the road. Royal Navy Sea Hawks were quickly summoned by radio; they struck in rapid succession at the buildings and completed the destruction begun by the Wyverns a while earlier.

At 10.30, the ground attack aircraft were also called in to carry out close support as a preliminary to the assault on the enemy. While Sea Hawks and Sea Venoms dived overhead, raking the enemy positions with gunfire, the troops left the cover of the reeds and raced across the open ground as far as the cemetery wall. Pouring over it they became engaged in a short and bloody hand-to-hand encounter with the defenders before the latter were overwhelmed. The paratroops killed thirty enemy soldiers and captured an old Bren-gun carrier for no casualties to themselves.

This action left the paratroops in command of the cemetery area, and they now pushed out patrols towards the flats and the Coastguard barracks. The patrols reported no opposition; in fact, the road into Port Said appeared to be wide open. The only problem was that by this time the paratroops were running dangerously short of ammunition; they had only fifty mortar bombs between them, and although Colonel Crook was aware that a further drop from Cyprus was scheduled for later that day, he decided not to risk a further advance – particularly since the objective areas were due to be bombarded by the Anglo-French Naval Task Force before the end of the day.

The paratroops accordingly spent the afternoon digging in and forming defensive positions on the sewage farm and airfield. Secure in these, they spent an uneventful night, punctuated only by some highly inaccurate mortar fire. A number of casualties had been sustained during the morning's fighting; these were quickly evacuated by Whirlwind helicopters from the carriers *Bulwark* and *Albion*. Another arrival at Gamil, while the battle was still going on, was a French Air Force C-47, whose pilot made a hair-raising landing between the oil drums that were still dotted around the airfield. The aircraft carried Colonel Becq de Fouquieres, a member of Admiral Barjot's staff, who had been sent to find out if it would be possible to fly French reinforcements into Gamil. For the medical team with the paratroops, the aircraft's arrival was a godsend; when it took off again it carried a number of the more serious casualties, who could now receive urgent hospital treatment in Cyprus. The surprising fact, however, is that no reinforcements were flown in by the *63eme Escadre*'s C-47s from Tymbou, and that this potential advantage was not exploited.

The medical staff at Gamil consisted of the 3rd Parachute Battalion's medical officer with a small staff of orderlies and stretcher-bearers, a section of the 23rd parachute Field Ambulance, and a field surgical team comprising one RAMC surgeon, one anaesthetist and four orderlies. Two field ambulances, followed by two casualty clearing stations and a mobile general hospital, were to land in the wake of the seaborne forces.

It was thought that the medical team parachuted into Gamil would be adequate to cope with the anticipated casualties of the airborne battalion during the first phase of the ground offensive; these were expected to be some 5 per cent of the force involved, a figure based on combat experience over a similar period in North-West Europe during the latter part of 1944. During the Suez airborne operation, however, a number of factors combined

94

to make the estimated casualty figure unrealistic. First of all, the French paratroops at Raswa lost a good deal of their medical kit during the air drop, which meant that the more serious cases among the casualties sustained that day had to be sent to Gamil for treatment by the British doctors before being evacuated. There were also substantial numbers of Egyptian wounded to be considered – all of which meant that the medical team, operating under primitive conditions and sometimes under fire, had an overwhelming burden to bear. To complicate matters still further, the 3rd Battalion's medical officer had been hit in the eye during his parachute descent; despite very severe pain, he continued working for more than four hours. He was eventually relieved by a Royal Navy surgeon lieutenant, who arrived with the first wave of helicopters.

Meanwhile, at Raswa, a detachment composed of men from the 9th Independent Squadron Royal Engineers and the Guards Parachute Company under Captain de Klee, who had dropped with the French paras, were making an armed reconnaissance south along the road between Kantara and Ismailia to investigate the possibility of an advance in that direction. Because of the geographical situation of Port Said, the routes leading inland were very limited from the tactical point of view, being exposed and highly vulnerable. Apart from the Suez Canal and the railway there were only two exits from the town, running parallel to the railway until one of them branched off twenty-five miles inland at Kantara. The Sweetwater Canal also ran along this narrow defile, between the railway and the minor of the two roads. But Klee and his men, to their surprise, found the road unmined for at least the first six miles of its course.

The Raswa bridges themselves presented the first potential obstacle to a drive on Suez, and the reconnaissance party's first task was to establish whether the bridges would be adequate for the transport and armour that would soon be passing over them. The engineers soon hit upon a snag; they found that the road bridge was two feet narrower than had been expected, which meant that it would have to be widened before it could be negotiated by Centurion tanks. Their inspection of the bridge was carried on with sporadic fighting still going on around them. As soon as the fighting was over, and the bridges firmly in the hands of the paras, the party set off along the Suez road to a point six miles south of Raswa, on the edge of the Anglo-French bomb line. They did not venture beyond this point for fear of being mistaken for Egyptians by the fighter-bomber pilots. The party found that although the road was free from mines, it was littered with a number of wrecked vehicles and there were some minor craters that later proved to be hazards during the advance towards Suez. Ample evidence was found that the Egyptians had in fact intended to destroy the road, but the Allied attack had apparently taken them by surprise because the explosives they had amassed for the purpose were found in a building and captured.

After interrogating some Egyptian civilians, the reconnaissance party returned to Raswa. They reported that the road to Suez was apparently free, and that an armoured column should easily be able to push along the full extent of the Canal. In fact, if the column pushed on rapidly, with no hold-ups, it could be in Suez in six hours. However, according to other civilians, there was a large concentration of Egyptian tanks extending westwards along the beach from Port Said; if this were true the Allied armour would probably have a fight on its hands from the moment it landed, and an early breakout would be unlikely.

That afternoon, as was mentioned in the preceding chapter, supplies, ammunition and reinforcements were air-dropped to the troops at Gamil and Raswa. The French drop successfully sealed the fate of the Egyptian defenders in Port Fuad, many of whom abandoned everything and made frantic attempts to escape across the Canal to Port Said before they were surrounded. Those who stood and fought were quickly mopped up by the determined paras as the latter closed in on the Canal ferry, isolating Port Fuad completely. The French were supported throughout the operation by Corsairs from the *Arromanches*, circling overhead in their 'cab-ranks'.

While the French and British paratroops consolidated their gains and took an inventory of the stores that had been dropped to them, new developments were taking place behind the scenes. Shortly after midday, a representative of Port Said's local government telephoned Colonel Château-Jobert's headquarters in the waterworks with the information that the Egyptian commandant,

General Moguy, was prepared to negotiate a ceasefire if the Allied air attacks were called off. Château-Jobert at once contacted Brigadier Butler, who was about to set out by helicopter to visit his troops at Gamil, and a signal was sent to the Allied command ship HMS *Tyne* requesting a halt to the air strikes while ceasefire negotiations took place.

By late afternoon, Château-Jobert and Butler had jointly worked out a set of ceasefire terms and the two officers flew to Raswa by helicopter to deliver them personally to General Moguy, the Allied commanders emphasising that they were of a temporary nature and would have to be verified by higher authority. The meeting between the opposing sides was cold and tense: no one sat down. The Egyptian general asked that the water supply to the town be re-connected and that the Allies 'stop killing civilians'.

The terms, which among other points demanded that the Egyptian troops should lay down their arms and converge on designated assembly points at Gamil and Port Fuad, were immediately relayed to Cairo by the Egyptian general. To his amazement, Moguy was told that there could be no question of accepting any ceasefire: World War III had started, Russian aircraft had attacked London and Paris, and thousands of Soviet troops were on their way to Egypt. More pressure was put on the bewildered General Moguy by Anatoly Tchikov, the Soviet Consul in Port Said, who told him that the town would become 'another Stalingrad' to be defended at all costs until the arrival of massive Russian reinforcements, who would sweep the Anglo-French aggressors into the sea. Tchikov was so convincing in his argument that he persuaded Moguy to authorise Port Said's police to break open crates full of Russian 7.62 mm rifles, which had arrived by rail in the evening of 4 November, and distribute the weapons to anyone who cared to take part in the 'heroic defence'. This was to result in a considerable sniper problem for the Allied forces who later occupied the port, with anyone from soldiers to small boys taking pot-shots at them. Fortunately, the Egyptians caused far more damage to each other than to the soldiers, or for that matter to the 800 foreign civilians living in Port Said. For these it was a time of great anxiety, particularly as many of them lived in blocks of flats overlooking the invasion beaches. Soon after the beginning of the emergency, all foreign nationals were placed under house arrest; the Americans, Italians and Greeks were later allowed to leave and were evacuated from either Port Said or Alexandria by their own ships, but for the British and French who remained the prospect of being hauled from their homes and shot loomed larger with every passing hour. In many cases, privately owned radios had been seized by the Egyptians, and the civilians had no real idea of what was happening – although the loudspeakers that toured the streets, telling of nuclear attacks on London and Paris and the early arrival of Soviet troops – painted a picture that was hardly reassuring.

Two former RAF officers, Sidney Brisk and David Larcombe, who had been employed as civilian instructors to the Egyptian Air Force and interned at the beginning of the emergency, had a unique insight into the workings of the Egyptian military mind[14]:

> When the call to action came in October, there were certainly no more than 500 pilots in Egypt who were capable of flying operationally, and probably the total figure was more like 200. The shortage of trained pilots was evident from the fact that all the Egyptian instructors at the college were called up for squadron service the moment any trouble seemed to be brewing. The number of pilots capable of flying the Russian jet planes must have been very much smaller than 200, for the Egyptians had great difficulty in mastering the MiGs and Il-28s properly. When they found they could not get the planes down on the runway, their only solution was to make the runway longer. If this did not suffice, they made the runway longer still.
>
> Our opportunities for observing just what was going on began to be limited about March 1956. At that time we became aware that our movements were being watched and that we needed to be careful what remarks we passed in the company of Egyptians. We knew for a fact, however, that the MiGs were stationed at Fayid, Almaza and Cairo West. There were Il-28s at Cairo West and one or two at Inchas. But when the build-up of Russian planes at Cairo West airfield began to be too obvious to passers-by on the main road to Alexandria, the road was diverted so that travellers could no longer get within sighting distance of the airfield.

When the British ultimatum came, the first reaction of the Egyptians with whom we were working was one of frank disbelief. They were certain it was a bluff. Then when the RAF bombers appeared the Egyptians were completely shattered. If you ask why the Egyptian Air Force did not take to the air against the attackers, there is one simple answer: the RAF had played an ungentlemanly trick by launching their attack at night. And when the weather conditions were at all unfavourable, all flying was automatically cancelled. No flying was allowed to take place unless there was a doctor at the airfield.

After the British night attacks had stunned the Egyptians into inactivity, came the renewed daylight offensive at first light of dawn. We saw Egyptian pilots gazing into the sky at the British bombers and remarking wistfully that something should be done about them. But it never occurred to them to take to the air themselves. In fact, so chaotic was the communications system that there seemed to be no-one with the necessary authority to order the fighters to scramble.

When it became evident that the British threat was not bluff, the BBC broadcasts were listened to avidly. As soon as it was announced that a certain place was to be bombed, the Egyptians solidly moved out. During the bombing of Bilbeis, the villagers moved into the airfield and stole as much furniture and equipment as they could lay their hands on. Afterwards, when we asked one of our own cadets how this had happened and how the villagers had got past the sentries, we were told that all the airfield's personnel had been 'busy hiding'.

But the tragic thing is that, in spite of the obvious success of the air attacks, the Egyptians believed that they had won a great victory. Loudspeakers in the streets were pouring out propaganda day and night. The Egyptians were told that the RAF lost 185 aircraft during the raids, and the majority of the population believed it.'

Many Egyptians also believed the tale that Russian military aid was imminent, and that nuclear attacks on London and Paris had taken place. But although the Soviet Premier, Marshal Nikolai Bulganin, was making indirect threats about the use of atomic weapons, the threats were empty. In 1956 the USSR possessed no missiles of sufficient range to attack either London or Paris; the Il-28 'Beagle' tactical jet bomber was not configured to carry nuclear bombs; and the Tu-16 'Badger' was still undergoing operational trials, with very few squadrons having achieved initial operational capability. Only the elderly Tupolev Tu-4 piston-engined bomber, a copy of the American Boeing B-29, was capable of attacking targets in western Europe, and its chances of survival in an environment dominated by jet fighters were negligible.

However, the possibility of intervention by conventional Soviet forces remained, and the Pentagon took it seriously. On 5 November, the USAF Strategic Air Command's bomber force stepped up its state of alert and concentrated its Boeing KC-97 tanker task forces at key bases in the northern part of the United States and in Greenland, Newfoundland and Labrador. If necessary, SAC was ready to go to war.

CHAPTER TWELVE

ASSAULT FROM THE SEA

By dawn on 6 November, the British and French paratroops were well established in their respective objectives. The sporadic firing that had been going on throughout the night had at last died away, leaving a silence that was almost unreal.

Offshore, after six days at sea, the invasion fleet had reached its station in the early hours of the morning, having split into three columns, and at 04.00, following final briefings, the commandos began to take up their positions in the assembled landing craft, while the Whirlwinds and Sycamores of the Joint Helicopter Unit stood by to follow on; the word 'Experimental' had been quietly dropped from its designation, mainly for reasons of morale.

In accordance with political instructions from London, there were to be no further bombing attacks by the Valiants and Canberras, and the use of heavy naval guns was also to cease. In order to minimise Egyptian casualties, and to avoid unnecessary collateral damage to property, General Keightley issued firm instructions that the air and naval pre-assault fire plan was to be concentrated solely on known Egyptian defences.

At first light, thirty-two Venoms of the Akrotiri Wing, each carrying eight squash head rockets, took off from their Cyprus base with orders to attack and destroy a number of guns in concrete emplacements on the West Mole breakwater that ran north from Port Said. The attack was led by the officer commanding No 6 Squadron, Sqn Ldr P.C. Ellis, who acted as Master Bomber, directing the waves of Venoms on to their targets. His task was complicated by the fact that the combat area was covered by heavy cloud, extending from 15,000 to 37,000 feet; the pilots had to descend through this from their approach altitude, which taxed them severely and made co-ordinating the attack difficult. Only 50 per cent of the rockets hit the breakwater, but this proved enough to silence the gun batteries, which offered no resistance to the seaborne landings.

The Royal Navy's fighter-bombers then went into action with a 10-minute air strike on the beach. This was followed by a 45-minute bombardment of the landing beach area by 4.5-inch naval guns, the use of heavier-calibre weapons having been vetoed, after which the Sea Hawks and Sea Venoms returned for a final air strike. By this time the gun emplacements on the foreshore had been neutralised, and the landing area was partially obscured by smoke from burning beach huts. A denser column of smoke rose from a blazing petroleum dump some distance inland; it was to burn for several days. The conflagration was caused by a stray rocket from some French Corsairs that had been called up by the French at Raswa to deal with a troublesome SU-100 SP gun, which they did very effectively.

At 04.30, the invasion force's LSTs – their approach to Port Said preceded by minesweepers on each wing – opened their bow doors and disgorged the first wave of amphibious 'Buffalo' Tracked Landing Vehicles (LVTs), each carrying thirty troops and their equipment, which churned towards the beach at a steady speed of seven knots as the last air strike went in. The first assault force to hit the beach – Sierra Red, to the left of the Casino Pier – was No 40 Royal Marine Commando under Lt-Col D.G. Tweed, whose task was to advance along the Canal and link up with the French at Raswa. Five minutes later, Lt-Col P.O. Norcock's 42 Commando landed on Sierra Green beach, to the right of the pier; their job was to fight their way through the town, sealing off the southern exits in the vicinity of the Golf Course Camp and link up with Tweed's men, while 3 Para – which was in a position to provide a degree of covering fire during the seaborne landings – moved up from Gamil through Port Said's shanty town to complete the junction. At the same time, the French assault force, comprising the *1er Regiment Etranger Parachutistes* and three naval commando units, supported by a squadron of AMX light tanks, made an unopposed landing on the beaches of Port Fuad.

The first wave of British Commandos found that most of the Egyptians had abandoned their defensive positions, but as they advanced towards the buildings that lined the road beyond the beach they came under heavy fire from enemy troops occupying blocks of flats further to the rear, and a number of casualties were sustained. It was with considerable relief that the Commandos watched their armoured support begin to come ashore; this took the shape of fourteen Centurions of C Squadron, 6th Royal Tanks, deposited 150 yards offshore by their LCTs. The tanks, which had been specially waterproofed, had to have their waterproof coverings removed before they could go into action, which the crews achieved under enemy fire. By 05.30 the task was completed; four Centurions were attached to No 40 Commando and the rest to No 42.

With the benefit of armoured support, No 40 Commando set off along the waterfront towards the Arsenal Basin, Navy House Quay and the Abbas Hilmi Basin, where the seaborne element of the 16th Parachute Brigade was scheduled to go ashore. The advance was difficult, as there were roadblocks at every junction, well defended by automatic weapons. When the Commandos found themselves pinned down by one of these obstacles they sent forward a Centurion, which destroyed the block and then sprayed the roads branching off from the junction with heavy machine-gun fire, under cover of which the men were able to dash across the exposed street ends.

The men of No 42 Commando, working their way through narrow streets on the right flank, were also glad of the Centurions' support. As well as automatic fire, they had to contend with hand grenades thrown from the upper storeys of blocks of flats. Despite this opposition the Marines continued to advance steadily, clearing buildings as they went, and at 07.45 they reached the gasworks on the southern edge of the town, having captured Port Said's cold storage plant and power station en route.

Meanwhile, 3 Para advanced from the cemetery, capturing the badly damaged Coastguard Barracks and the Ophthalmic Hospital before moving into the slum suburb. Here, the paratroops encountered severe opposition; the first patrol was hit by heavy automatic fire and every man was wounded. Because of the close proximity of the opposing forces and the difficulty of identifying targets among the jumble of shanties, there was no possibility of calling in an air strike; instead, a 105 mm anti-tank gun and one of the destroyers offshore shelled the area, starting fires that were soon raging among the crowded buildings of the shanty town.

Seven miles out to sea, on the aircraft carriers HMS *Ocean* and HMS *Theseus*, the men of No 45 Commando received the news that the beach areas had been secured by Nos 40 and 42 Commandos, and a Whirlwind of No 845 Naval Air Squadron carrying Lt-Col Tailyour, Major De'Ath and three Marines was despatched to make a reconnaissance of the chosen LZ. The original one had been close to the statue of Ferdinand de Lesseps, but this had been changed because of its distance from Brigade HQ. When the reconnaissance party flew over the new LZ, however, they found it obscured by smoke, and the presence of high-tension wires provided an additional hazard. The Whirlwind pilot decided to land on the nearby Egyptian Stadium, taking off as soon as his passengers had disembarked.

Almost as soon as they left the helciopter, the reconnaissance party came under heavy fire from an Egyptian position on the far side of the stadium. The five men took refuge in the players' entrance and prepared to fight it out. Fortunately, the Whirlwind pilot, circling overhead, spotted their predicament and braved the enemy fire to land back on the stadium. His passengers dashed across 200 yards of open ground and scrambled into the helicopter, which got away despite sustaining twenty-two hits. The pilot was slightly wounded, but he managed to locate another landing zone, a rubble-strewn patch of waste ground to the west of the de Lesseps statue. This was judged to be suitable for a landing, and shortly before 06.00 Tailyour sent a radio message ordering No 45 Commando's mission to proceed.

The Joint Helicopter Unit (JHU), which was commanded by an Army officer, Lt Col J.F.T. Scott TD, had six Whirlwind Mk 2s and six Sycamores, all of which had been stripped of unnecessary equipment so that the maximum number of Commandos – five in the Whirlwind and three in the Sycamore – could be carried. The operation was to be executed in conjunction with the ten Whirlwinds of No 845 Squadron.

The helicopters approached the LZ in waves. On arrival overhead, each wave orbited while individual helicopters broke away to make a rapid touchdown and disembark the men, all the while under sniper fire. One man was hit almost immediately; he was hauled back on board the helicopter and was being treated in *Ocean*'s sick bay a bare twenty minutes after he had first left the carrier. As the airlift continued, returning helicopters picked up casualties – some of them Egyptian – at the LZ and flew them back to the carriers. One Whirlwind of 845 Squadron, badly hit by enemy fire, had to ditch forty yards away from *Theseus*, but its crew and the three wounded Marines it carried were picked up safely by a launch.

By 06.30, the shuttling helicopters had landed No 45 Commando's E and Z Troops, Tactical Headquarters, anti-tank detachments and an Air Contact Team whose task it was to liaise with the close support aircraft patrolling overhead. During the next couple of hours all the Commando's Rifle Troops, including the Support Troop and equipment – a total of 425 men and 23 tons of stores – were brought ashore by the Whirlwinds and Sycamores. It had been the first assault of its kind in history, and its success had certainly vindicated the concept – a concept due entirely to the initiative of a senior naval officer, Vice-Admiral Sir Guy Sayer, the Flag Officer Home Fleet Training Squadron, whose brainchild it was.

The contribution made to the airlift by JHU, with its lower carrying capacity, was quite remarkable. Led by Sqn Ldr D.C.L. Kearns AFC, the unit's second in command, the helicopters ferried 178 men and 12.5 tons of stores from HMS *Ocean* in the first two and a half hours, as well as evacuating casualties. Kearns was awarded the Distinguished Service Cross.

Later in the day, JHU helicopters flew personnel of No 215 Wing RAF (Group Captain W.V. Crawford-Compton DSO DFC) from HMS *Ocean* to Gamil, where the runway was found to be suitable for transport aircraft. Signals personnel and equipment were brought in by Valetta, while the helicopters flew in an advance party of No 48 (Field) Squadron, RAF Regiment under Sqn Ldr J.E.S. Wilson. The rest of the Squadron arrived within 24 hours, and assumed the task of airfield defence.

As soon as they had landed, the Commandos of E Troop, under Major Leslie Marsh, set out to clear some blocks of flats in the vicinity of the LZ so that the Commandos could use

105

this position for its assembly area. The men worked their way through the buildings, killing several snipers with small arms fire and grenades, and by 07.00 the flats were secure. An hour later, E and Z Troop led the Commando towards the centre of Port Said, where it was to capture and hold the broad avenue of Shari el Mahrousa and the Governorate building. This was a rambling, colonial-style structure set in magnificent gardens, which provided an excellent field of fire for the Egyptian snipers who were sheltering there. After a brief fire-fight the snipers were eliminated by E Troop, but almost immediately afterwards the Egyptians laid down more fire from a position further up the road, halting the advance of Z Troop.

While E and Z Troops were engaging the snipers, the Commando's Tactical HQ, followed by A, B and X Troops, were approaching the northern end of Shari el Mahrousa, the troops advancing cautiously and on the alert for snipers. As they did so, they were suddenly attacked by a Westland Wyvern fighter-bomber, whose pilot, it transpired later, had been given an erroneous map reference for his air strike target. The aircraft's cannon shells wounded Lt-Col Tailyour in the arm and fatally wounded his signaller, Marine Michael Fowler; Lieutenant John Weston, 45 Commando's Intelligence Officer, and fourteen other ranks were also injured. To make matters worse, all the Marines' radio sets were damaged in the attack, so that contact with the forward troops was lost for some time. The casualties were evacuated to the LZ in an ambulance provided by 40 Commando, while the Tactical HQ was quickly reorganised. Major Richard Crombie took over from the injured Tailyour, while Lt-Cdr Lionel Jenkins assumed the role of Intelligence Officer.

Meanwhile, in its sector, Z Troop was encountering stiff resistance as it advanced past the Governorate Building, as the Troop Report tells:

> Almost immediately 19 Section (Sgt Saxton) and 18 Section (Sgt Fellows) suffered casualties from snipers in a large white building. 18 Section had Marine K. Essau hit in the leg and L/Cpl M.T. Porter in the back. 19 Section had Marine Cyril Goodfellow killed and Marine Smith shot in the arm. 17 Section

(Sgt Smith) had two casualties from an enemy on the top floor, Cpl J.F. Rutherford shot in the leg, and Marine Cowling. The luckiest escape was Marine McLeod who had the lion shot off the badge on his beret, but he was unhurt. E Troop then moved forward from the area of the gardens to give support.

The fighting around Shari el Mahrousa was also described in 45 Commando's Battle Report:

The buildings along Shari el Mahrousa were in general seven-storey blocks of concrete or brick flats, the ground floors consisting of shops protected by steel shutters. Inside the buildings narrow stairways gave access upwards. The houses were occupied by civilians, with children. Egyptian army and police, many disguised in plain clothes, fought furiously. Some prisoners were found to have Benzedrine tablets in their possession. Many enemy wearing plain clothes fought until the last moment, and then discarding their weapons, posed as civilian refugees. In general the enemy defence was not co-ordinated, but groups of riflemen and machine-gunners hotly contested any advance. In two instances enemy snipers committed suicide rather than be captured. To offset the lack of tanks a 106 mm anti-tank gun was set up on a borrowed carrier and used to blast a way through steel shutters and concrete walls. By this means the assault troops were used to effect an entry.

At 09.15 B Troop (Capt Richard Meadows), which had seven men wounded in the air strike, moved forward to assist the forward troops. The Troop reformed to four sections and remained in the first block on the west side of the Shari el Mahrousa from where they shot along the streets going west, thereby covering the movement of our own troops up the main axis of advance. Z Troop asked for assistance to clear a sniper who was preventing them from evacuating wounded. Sgt Cooper's section cleared the sniper with the aid of an Energa bomb (an anti-tank bomb fired from a rifle grenade launcher), which was very effective in this role, and then covered the removal of wounded. The Troop Sergeant Major, Kennedy, and Marine Connelly . . . together with Marines Galley, Morris and Watson in the Bren Group, killed a considerable number of enemy moving 200yd along one of the roads going west from the Shari el Mahrousa. The enemy were endeavouring to remove a small gun from its position in the middle of a road.

By 11.00 the Commandos had cleared the Shari el Mahrousa area. Leaving behind some Marines in the buildings to deal with possible Egyptian infiltrators, the remainder swung westwards towards the shanty town, where they were to link up with 3 Para. Supported by Centurion tanks, the Commandos advanced through stiff opposition and at 14.30 reached Shari el Sherrif, a road running laterally across their path. Here, Z Troop encountered strong resistance as they cleared the houses, the men dodging grenades thrown at them from the upper storeys. The Egyptians were eventually dislodged by a Centurion, which bombarded them from point-blank range with its main armament. The Marines pushed on, and at 16.00 they reached their second main objective, the avenue of Shari el Ghazi Moukhtar. Here, with contact not yet established with the Paras, they halted and prepared defensive positions as an insurance against an Egyptian counter-attack during the night. In the day's fighting No 45 Commando had killed an estimated 150 Egyptians; their own losses amounted to three men killed and thirty wounded.

No 40 Commando, meanwhile, which earlier had passed rapidly through the area cleared by No 45, had reached their first main objective, the Commercial Basin, at 15.00 and occupied the offices of the Suez Canal Company. Their next objective, the nearby Customs Warehouse, was strongly defended, and in their attempts to take it the Marines lost two officers killed and three men wounded. Again, Centurion tanks shelled the building for several minutes, after which the Commandos were able to mop up the defenders.

The Navy House, a massive stone structure next door that had been the Royal Navy's HQ in Port Said before the British withdrawal, proved an even tougher nut to crack. It was defended by 130 well-armed and determined Egyptian soldiers, and after several costly and unsuccessful attempts to storm the building the Marines withdrew and called in an air strike. A flight of Sea Hawks arrived shortly before dusk and made rocket attacks on the building, which was occupied the next morning. Many of the defenders had got away under cover of darkness, but 30 were dead and 20 surrendered to the Commandos.

While a proportion of the Royal Navy's strike aircraft had been detailed to fly close support missions as required during the day, others had joined the RAF Venoms of the Akrotiri Wing on armed reconnaissance. During these excursions, No 6 Squadron destroyed an ammunition dump at El Kantara and three fire engines and two fuel bowsers at Abu Sueir.

The day's operations cost the Royal Navy a Sea Hawk and a Wyvern. The pilot of the latter, an aircraft of HMS *Eagle*'s No 830 Squadron, ejected at 8,000 feet over the Suez Canal when his engine caught fire near Ismailia. While a flight of French Navy Corsairs provided CAP overhead, he set out to walk to Israeli-held territory, but before he reached it he was picked up by a Whirlwind rescue helicopter from HMS *Bulwark*. The Sea Hawk pilot, Lieutenant Donald Mills of 897 Squadron, was shot down during an attack on the military camp at Kantara; he too landed by parachute in the desert on the eastern side of the Canal and was rescued by helicopter.

In the afternoon, one of No 6 Squadron's pilots, Flying Officer Budd, sighted a swept-wing aircraft engaged in strafing Gamil airfield. He went in pursuit and got to within 500 yards of it, but the aircraft easily out-ran his Venom. It was a MiG-15, and it carried Russian markings.

This fact caused considerable excitement, not to say alarm, for reports of an apparent Soviet military build-up in Syria were continuing to reach the Allied Expeditionary Force HQ. Most of them were false, and stemmed from events of 2 November, when the French CCFO (*Commandant en Chef des Forces Francaises d'Orient*) had been informed by GHQ in Paris that the Syrian Government had declared a state of emergency, and that foreign aircraft were forbidden to fly over Syrian territory until further notice. This was quickly followed by another report stating that Soviet freighters had unloaded 100 tanks and 120 artillery pieces at the Syrian port of Latakia.

At 14.22 on 6 November, a signal reached Allied Command in Cyprus from NATO Supreme Allied Command in Europe indicating that unidentified jet traffic, apparently heading for Syria or Egypt, had been detected passing through Turkish air space at high altitude. The Turkish Air Force was placed on full alert, and in the course of the afternoon Hunters from Nicosia were scrambled to investigate a suspicious radar contact 50 miles north of Cape Andreas. At a little over 50,000 feet, the Hunter pilots made visual contact with the suspect aircraft, which was several thousand feet above them, and made a positive identification. It was a Lockheed U-2, the aircraft behind all the panic. Operating out of Incirlik in Turkey in the greatest secrecy, it had been engaged in photographic reconnaissance sorties over Syria and the Canal Zone for several days. Its operations were CIA-controlled, and the CIA had not told NATO what was going on.

On 6 November, No 13 Squadron despatched several Canberra PR sorties to Syria to ascertain what was really happening. On one of these, Canberra PR7 WH799 was intercepted by a Syrian Air Force Meteor NF13 and shot down. The navigator, Fg Off Urquhart-Pullen, was killed; the pilot, Flt Lt Hunter, and a third crew member, baled out over the Lebanese border and survived. They were detained in Beirut Military Hospital for a spell before being repatriated.

There was a further panic when, at 15.00 GMT on the 6th, the French Defence Department received intelligence from a 'reliable source' that Russian submarines had been sighted on the approaches to Alexandria, and at 15.40 an urgent signal arrived at Episkopi from London stating that 'Russia may take part in Middle East with force'. At 18.05, a top secret signal from Paris warned Admiral Barjot 'to prepare the Fleet for defensive and offensive action against Soviet aircraft and warships'.

But the submarines were not Russian. They were American boats, the USS *Cutlass* and *Hardhead*, back in the invasion area to observe what was going on.

In the French sector, meanwhile, everything had gone according to plan. At Raswa, the French were guarding their positions to the south of the town and waiting for the arrival of the British; they had lost two men killed, but in return had killed or captured seventy-two Egyptians and taken a large amount of equipment, including six anti-tank guns. The French badly needed heavy armoured support, having been under attack by SU-100 self-propelled guns since the Egyptian rejection of the

Allied ceasefire proposal the previous evening. The Raswa bridges were the only means of escape for the Egyptian forces trapped in Port Said, and enemy forces from the south made several attempts to recapture them, although their efforts were frustrated by air strikes.

The promised armoured support eventually arrived in the shape of the Centurions of A Squadron, 6th RTR, which were offloaded at Port Said's Casino Wharf at 08.30. The tanks moved off through the area cleared by 40 Commando and reached the French a little late, having become bogged down on the golf course, but all were assembled at Raswa by 12.00. B Squadron of 6 RTR and the Regimental HQ were also landed later in the day by the LSTs *Salerno* and *Puncher*.

By nightfall on 6 November, fourteen LSTs had unloaded their cargoes of troops, vehicles and stores either at the Casino Wharf or at Port Said's Fishing Harbour, while more reinforcements came ashore from troopships, which entered the Inner Harbour as soon as it was declared free of mines. Among the first reinforcements to land were the men of the 16th Parachute Brigade Group, who were scheduled to drive on to Ismailia. The 2nd Parachute Battalion led the way off the troopship *Empire Parkeston*, followed by an advance party of the Guards Independent Parachute Company and supporting vehicles, the whole force setting off to join the French at Raswa. There was still a lot of sniper fire, but for the most part it was inaccurate and the snipers were quickly dealt with by the Paras and by Marines positioned at various key points.

The paratroops reached Raswa at 19.00 hours and regrouped in readiness for the drive to Ismailia. Centurions of A Squadron, 6 RTR, accompanied by French Paras, had already set out to make a reconnaissance, and reported that they had reached the Suez Canal Company's radio station at El Tina without meeting any opposition. There they halted to await the arrival of the main force. The plan now was to drive on to Ismailia at first light, the land column being supported if necessary by two more French airborne landings: one by Colonel Bigeard's 3 RPC at Kantara, and the other by Colonel Meyer's 1 RPC near Ismailia iself.

The Allied commanders were anxious to complete this operation as quickly as possible, but they were to be thwarted by political events. At 18.00, in response to repeated ceasefire demands by the United Nations Secretary-General, the British Government indicated that, pending confirmation that hostilities had ceased between Egyptian and Israeli forces and that a United Nations force would be sent into the combat area, British forces in Egypt would be ordered to cease fire with effect from midnight unless they were attacked. Anthony Eden had already telephoned the French Premier, Guy Mollet, and announced the Government's decision; Mollet, despite pressure from his cabinet, refused to continue without Britain's support.

Although the commanders in the field had received a signal from General Keightley indicating that a ceasefire was in the offing, their only confirmation of it was on the BBC news at nine o'clock. They received the report with some scepticism; even if a ceasefire did come into force, there was no guarantee that it would not be broken later, and if such proved to be the case neither Brigadier Butler, commanding the 16th Parachute Brigade, nor his counterpart General Jacques Massu, commanding the French column, thought it advisable for their forces to remain sitting astride the narrow causeway leading south from Port Said. Neither did General Stockwell, the Land Task Force Commander, who immediately ordered Butler to proceed with all speed to El Cap, at the far end of the causeway twenty-five miles from Port Said. Butler's aim, however, was to push on as far as El Kantara, seven miles further on.

By 23.00 the column was on the move again, the Centurions, raising a huge cloud of dust in the moonlight, followed by 2 Para, travelling in every kind of vehicle they had been able to lay hands on. Eventually, the tanks rumbled into El Cap. In the distance, the crews could see the lights of Kantara, almost within reach, but Brigadier Butler had no alternative other than to call a halt. It was 00.20 GMT, and the ceasefire had already been in force for twenty minutes.

Chapter Thirteen

Occupation

First light on 7 November found the paratroops at El Cap still digging in on either side of the 250-yard wide causeway, flanking anti-tank rifles and machine-guns that had been set up to cover the ground ahead. The Centurions were deployed farther to the rear, their armament trained on Egyptian defensive positions that had been sighted some distance in front. These had been abandoned but appeared to be intact, and if the ceasefire should be broken they could easily be reoccupied by enemy troops, some of whom had been sighted among trees about a mile away. After a while the enemy force, which was about fifty strong, began to move in the direction of the forward British positions. The paratroops, with orders to open fire only if they were attacked, could do nothing but wait to see what might happen. Then a group of Egyptians closed to within fifty yards and fired several shots, one of which wounded a member of one of the tank crews. On the orders of the tank commander, the Centurion's gunner, who had been covering the Egyptians with his machine-gun, opened fire and killed two of them. The others ran off and escaped in some trucks. All were wearing civilian clothing.

There was a further alarm when, early in the afternoon, clouds of dust betrayed the movement of enemy transport in the desert south of the causeway, and a build-up of vehicles was seen among the trees from which the first attack had developed. A Whirlwind helicopter, summoned to make a reconnaissance, was fired on, but its crew stayed in the vicinity long enough to confirm that the enemy vehicles included armour. To guard against a possible enemy attack, the paratroops set about strengthening their positions with railway sleepers. Brigadier Butler alerted the Air Task Force that air support might be needed, a possibility that loomed

113

large when, late in the afternoon, air reconnaissance indicated a
build-up of T-34 tanks and SU-100 SP guns north of Ismailia.
In the event nothing happened, and there was no resumption
of hostilities, which was just as well, for the drawdown of the
supporting Allied air and naval forces had already begun.

In the afternoon of 7 November, HMS *Eagle* and her air group
of six squadrons sailed for Malta; her port catapult, which had
made 631 launches during the operation, was the worse for
wear and needed attention. Vice-Admiral Manley Power, the
Carrier Task Force Commander, and his staff were transferred
by helicopter to HMS *Bulwark*. Also on 7 November, three
Valiant squadrons, Nos 138, 148 and 207, left Malta to return
to their UK bases, while in the next 24 hours three Canberra
squadrons, Nos 10, 15 and 44, departed Nicosia for the United
Kingdom. As a precaution against renewed hostilities, however,
20 Valiants and 24 Canberras continued to be held at varying
states of readiness in the United Kingdom, and all shore-based
aircraft remaining in the Mediterranean remained at their
Musketeer locations, releasing the Royal Navy's carrier-borne
aircraft. Following these redeployments, air operations in the
eastern Mediterranean were limited to photographic and tactical reconnaissance and transport support, the latter assuming
great significance with the continuing presence of British and
French troops in and around Port Said and the occupation of
Gamil.

In Port Said itself street fighting and sniping still continued,
mainly because many Egyptians were unaware of the ceasefire.
So far, Cairo Radio had made no mention of it. Mopping
up the remaining pockets of resistance proceeded at dawn
on 7 November, after 3 Para at last joined up with No 45
Commando. By the end of the day, the latter had seized
fifty-seven 3-ton truckloads of weapons and ammunition,
the small-arms ranging from old 1914-model British Lee-
Enfield .303 rifles to modern Czech carbines. Any Russian
or Czech equipment was retained for evaluation; the rest was
rendered harmless and placed in a compound for eventual
dumping at sea. A search of the shanty town the next day
turned up more quantities of arms, most of which had
been smuggled into Port Said on fishing boats. The boats

were also used in attempts to evacuate Egyptian troops out of the town via the Manzala Canal, but this ceased when Allied troops instituted regular inspections of the dhows.

In the meantime, two more flights of No 48 (Field) Squadron RAF Regiment had been flown into Gamil from HMS *Ocean*, and the Squadron now went into the line to relieve A Company of 3 Para on the east side of the airfield. During the night, the remaining obstacles having been cleared from the landing area, six Valettas arrived from Cyprus laden with jerrycans of urgently-needed water. They were unloaded by the headlights of Land-Rovers and were on their way again within an hour and twenty minutes. As the historian of the RAF in the Mediterranean puts it: 'With Group Captain Crawford-Compton marshalling the aircraft and his second in command, Wing Commander M.H. Le Bas DSO AFC, as air traffic controller, the Gamil aircraft handling party had decidedly top heavy characteristics.'

One principal concern, while clearance operations continued, was to restore Port Said's public utilities as quickly as possible. To this end, Royal Engineers began work on the main power station and the waterworks at Raswa in the afternoon of 7 November. The plants themselves had sustained only minor damage, but their distribution systems had been seriously disrupted and it would need at least a week's work before they could be brought fully into action again. The sewage system was completely unreliable and kept breaking down, which turned Port Said into a highly unsavoury environment and created a serious health hazard that was of great concern to Royal Army Medical Corps personnel, who had set up temporary hospitals in hotels and other prominent buildings to deal with casualties. British and French Army doctors were also soon at work in the Egyptian hospitals, which were allocated medical supplies as soon as these were brought ashore in sufficient quantities. On 9 November an American Red Cross train, the first of several, arrived from Cairo, having passed the point where the British and Egyptians were still in confrontation at El Cap without incident, and evacuated some 200 wounded to the Egyptian capital.

The British proceeded cautiously with the occupation of Port Said, alert for trouble at every street corner. However, once the more fanatical pockets of resistance had been dealt with, the average Egyptian civilian showed little sign of hostility towards the occupying forces; indeed, many came forward with offers of assistance. The real bugbear was Radio Cairo, which continued to hurl out virulent propaganda; encouraged by this, subversive elements in Port Said, actively supported by the Soviet consul, embarked on a growing campaign of terror. The threat to the lives of senior British personnel was very real; General Stockwell and other senior officers had to be accompanied by armed parties wherever they went. Egyptians known to be collaborating with the occupying forces were murdered and had their homes burned, with the result that civilian working parties employed in the docks and elesewhere refused to co-operate any longer. Looting increased, and despite the efforts of foot patrols to enforce a curfew armed terrorists appeared on the streets and sporadic sniping once again became a problem. As part of the move to deal with infractions of the ceasefire, helicopters of the JHU and Austers of No 1913 Light Liaison Flight, flown in from Cyprus, flew policing sorties on request over Port Said during November, accounting for many of the 266 aircraft sorties handled by No 215 Wing at Gamil between the ceasefire and 26 November. (The total included 52 Hastings and 125 Valetta flights.)

The French had less of a problem, as General Beaufre explains[15]:

> The first and most urgent requirement was re-establishment of law and order. In the French zone this was assured from the outset thanks to the agreement reached with the police by Lt-Col Fossey-Francois when Port Fuad was taken. All houses had been searched, suspects arrested and weapons confiscated. The Egyptian police remained armed and the shops reopened. There was not a single attack on persons. As soon as any minor incident took place, punishment followed at once . . . I declared that 'resisters' should be regarded as combatants (in accordance with the Geneva Convention) and they were treated as prisoners

116

of war; generally they were released fairly quickly but threatened with deportation to France. Since, moreover, electricity and water supply had been re-established from the outset and food supply was assured (we distributed it), the atmosphere was good, even cordial, in spite of Cairo Radio. Port Fuad was of course a far easier proposition than Port Said, but I am convinced that similar methods would have succeeded there also.

On the morning of Sunday 10 November, the troopships *New Australia, Empire Fowey* and *Asturias* arrived in the eastern Mediterranean after an eight-day voyage from the United Kingdom and joined units of the Allied fleet five miles off the Egyptian coast. The ships carried the leading echelons of General Churcher's 3rd Division, comprising the 19th and 29th Infantry Brigades supported by the 1st Royal Tanks. The task of ferrying these occupation troops ashore began within 24 hours, and their arrival made it possible to begin the phased withdrawal of the Commando and paratroop units that had taken part in the invasion. The paratroops were to pull out as far as Cyprus, where they were to remain on standby until further notice; air reconnaissance had revealed that the Egyptians were rapidly repairing some of their key airfields in the Canal Zone, and there was still a possibility that hostilities might break out once more if the Russians or Czechs supplied combat aircraft. The danger was highlighted by the fact that the Egyptians at El Cap had reoccupied all their defensive positions and were now sending out reconnaissance patrols right up to the Allied line, where the opposing sides still exchanged occasional bursts of gunfire. On 11 November, the 1st Battalion Royal West Kents disembarked and moved up to this tense area, where they relieved 2 Para.

The day before, while the 3rd Division prepared to move ashore, the first troops of the United Nations Expeditionary Force destined for Egypt – 51 Danish soldiers – were airlifted to Naples by a USAF Douglas C-124 Globemaster. Similar aircraft also picked up Norwegian troops in Oslo and brought them to Naples, where arrangements were made to ferry them to Egypt aboard Swissair DC-6Bs. Several UN observers arrived in Port Said on the 11th, ahead of the main contingent, and travelled to El Cap, where they visited both Allied and Egyptian commanders.

On 13 November, the Royal Fusiliers came ashore at Port Said and relieved 3 Para, while the 1st Royal Scots took control of No 45 Commando's area of responsibility. No 45 Commando, together with 40 Commando and Brigade HQ, embarked on the troopship *Empire Fowey* the next day and sailed for Malta, arriving on the 17th. On 15 November, two companies of the Argyll and Sutherland Highlanders arrived to take over perimeter defence and patrol duties at Gamil airfield; No 48 (Field) Squadron RAF Regiment was then redeployed, with a Flight on the east bank of the Manzala Canal, another midway between the Canal and the airfield, and a tactical HQ and a reserve Flight behind them, so that the western approaches to the airfield were covered.

On the 21st the Royal Fusiliers moved up to El Cap to relieve the Royal West Kents, and a week later they were relieved in turn by the 1st Battalion, the York and Lancaster Regiment. The latter was still there when, on 30 November, two companies of Danish UN troops arrived by train from Abu Sueir. Transfer of responsibility to the Danes was completed on 7 December, and the next day the York and Lancasters went to Port Said to embark on HMS *Theseus* for the voyage home to the United Kingdom.

CHAPTER FOURTEEN

THE TROOPS DEPART

Despite the arrival of the United Nations force in Egypt, there was still a great deal of uncertainty about the future of the Anglo-French military forces that remained. Everything now depended on a satisfactory political compromise, and if no such compromise could be reached, there was always the possibility that arrangements would have to be made for a lengthy stay in Port Said, with the occupation of the entire Canal Zone a possibility. In fact, it was not until 3 December that definitive plans were laid for a complete withdrawal.

At the beginning of December 1956 the Port Said garrison consisted of the 19th Infantry Brigade – comprising the Royal Scots, the West Yorkshire Regiment, and the Argyll and Sutherland Highlanders – and two regiments of the 29th Brigade, the Royal Fusiliers and the Royal West Kents. The British troops were assisted by 800 Egyptian police, while a further 350, brought in from Cairo, worked alongside the United Nations force. At Port Fuad, the French maintained one brigade comprising the *1er Regiment Parachutistes Coloniaux* and the *1er Regiment Etranger Parachutistes* supported by a squadron of AMX tanks.

Although the French-occupied areas remained generally quiet, the French having made it quite clear how they would deal with transgressors, this was far from true in Port Said, particularly in the Arab Town, which lay in the Royal Scots' sector. Here, grenade-throwing attacks and shootings, which had been little more than isolated incidents at first, suddenly developed into something far more serious, and there seemed to be a growing degree of co-ordination behind the activity. Although Cairo Radio was being jammed on General Stockwell's orders, the flames of unrest were fanned by a growing underground

119

movement in Port Said, which continued to flourish despite a British proclamation threatening severe penalties for anyone caught intimidating Egyptians who were eager to co-operate with the occupying power.

Allied to this upsurge in urban terrorist activity was the worrying fact that the Egyptians had taken full advantage of the ceasefire to consolidate their military position in Kantara and Ismailia; if the Allied advance along the Canal had to be resumed for any reason, securing these objectives would mean much heavy fighting, and probably considerable cost in human life. General Keightley, having visited the area earlier, was particularly concerned about the rise of a strong and fanatical resistance movement in Port Said and in the Egyptian army itself. There was no doubt, he said, that both in fighting spirit and in equipment the Egyptian army was much improved[16]:

> I have been considering the situation if we are required to continue the operation. I would say with all emphasis that we must not be required to do this unless we can have and use every weapon we require. Without bombing, for instance, we shall now clearly not break the Egyptian wish to resist and we can no longer fight with the warnings and care for property which we have exercised so far. If we try to do so, the war will be prolonged and our casualties high.

Since the Allied commanders were aware that the street violence in Port Said was likely to escalate considerably as the date for the evacuation approached, the latter was kept a closely guarded secret. Nevertheless, as December wore on the street attacks increased in their savagery. On the 10th, an officer of the West Yorkshire Regiment, 2nd Lt Moorhouse, was kidnapped and murdered by terrorists. It later appeared that they had intended to hold him to ransom, but that he had suffocated when they had locked him, bound and gagged, in a metal trunk. In another incident an Egyptian policeman was shot dead, and a major in the Royal Scots fatally wounded when a patrol was ambushed. On 15 December, the biggest clash since the ceasefire occurred when a large band of armed terrorists roamed through the streets of the Arab Town. On General Stockwell's orders troops were sent in to quell the disturbance, supported by Centurion tanks, and thirty Egyptians were killed or wounded in the ensuing skirmish.

By 20 December the total number of United Nations troops in Egypt stood at 6,000, made up of contingents from Denmark, Sweden, Norway, Colombia, Finland, Indonesia, Yugoslavia and India, under the overall command of the Canadian General E.L.M. 'Tommy' Burns. A Canadian contingent had been proposed for the force, but had been rejected forcefully by Nasser; Canadians wore the same uniform as the British, had the same Queen, and had similar regimental titles.

The first task of the UN troops was to provide a buffer between the Egyptian and British forces at El Cap, enabling the British to pull back along the causeway. The United Nations force would then begin to assume gradual responsibility for Port Said, providing guards for vital installations and ensuring, as far as possible, that the administration of the area continued to function while the Allied evacuation took place. The plan was for the British and French forces to assemble within a perimeter close to the entrance to the Canal, separated from the rest of the port by a barbed wire fence. On 20 December, the RAF, which had in the meantime cleaned up Gamil airfield and restored it to full working order, handed over their responsibility to the Larsen Company of the UNEF's Danish battalion.

Because of the size of the Allied force, working out a timetable for the evacuation presented a great many problems. During the first week of December there were some 22,000 Allied troops in Port Said and the surrounding area, together with 4,800 vehicles and over 10,000 tons of stores and equipment, and it was estimated that about three weeks would be needed to evacuate them all. To add to the problem, several hundred Allied nationals would also have to be evacuated. British nationals included people of Maltese, Cypriot and Lebanese origin; many of them had lived in Egypt all their lives, and now they had lost everything. Under Military Law No 5, passed on 1 November, Nasser had sequestered all goods and property belonging to the British and French Governments, companies, institutions and private individuals. These included nine banks, sixty-four insurance companies and shares in a large number of other concerns.

Eventually, it was decided that the rearguard of the Allied force would consist of the 19th Brigade, a squadron of the 6th Royal Tanks, two battalions of the French Foreign Legion and a squadron of AMX tanks, together with a French naval detachment. The evacuation began in earnest on 7 December, and by the 14th more than 11,000 British troops had been taken out of Port Said on HMS *Theseus* and the troopships *Ascania* and *Dilwara*, priority being given to reservists and time-expired National Servicemen. They were closely followed by the contingent of Allied nationals, many of whom had been released at the very last moment in exchange for 250 of their own who had been held by the British and French. (The latter included General Moguy, who had been captured at an early stage in the campaign.)

The final evacuation was to take place on 22 December, by which time the remaining British and French forces had withdrawn behind their perimeter. The occasion was not without its emotion; the Union Flag still flew defiantly over the prominent buildings as the last British troops to leave took their stations near the Casino Palace Hotel, while over in Port Fuad the French troops marched past their commanders in full battle order, with colours flying, before making their way down to the main pier.

The French made no secret of their bitterness about the way in which the military operation had ended. For many officers, the sense of betrayal was so profound that their loyalty to their government was shaken. General Jacques Massu's hard-bitten Paras had obeyed the ceasefire of 6 November 'with rage in the heart . . . when Cairo seems to us just around the corner, with no serious obstacle to prevent our advance'. On his return to Algiers, Massu discovered that the FLN rebels had transformed Nasser's unexploited defeat into 'a triumphal victory. Not only do its faithful take heart, but those who had given over to panic want to reaffirm their loyalty . . . Our hearts are heavy'.

In both Port Said and Port Fuad, the last troops embarked at 17.00, and the codeword *Lobster* advised Allied HQ in Cyprus that the Anglo-French forces were now clear of Egyptian soil.

Operation *Musketeer* was over. But for some Anglo-French units, there was still a great deal of work to be done in Egypt. These were the Naval salvage teams which, operating under

United Nations control, now set about the task of clearing obstructions from the Suez Canal. There were plenty. In Port Said harbour alone there were twenty-four scuttled vessels of up to 3,600 tons, and the bottoms of most of them had been ripped out by explosions. The Egyptians had scuttled a further twenty-seven vessels along the length of the Canal between Port Said and Suez; these included tugs, dredgers, barges filled with concrete, salvage vessels and a tank landing craft. A few were completely submerged. The Egyptians had also blown the 165 foot railway bridge at El Ferdan, halfway down the Canal, and a pontoon bridge at the southern end of Lake Timsah. Sixteen freighters and tankers had been trapped in the Canal by the wrecks.

The British and French salvage operations, which in fact had begun soon after the Allied Expeditionary Force landed, were restricted to the part of the Canal that had been occupied and under Anglo-French control after the ceasefire. It was fortunate that Admiral Mountbatten, the First Sea Lord, had had the foresight to assemble a substantial salvage fleet, including six heavy lift vessels, at Cyprus before the invasion began; it meant that work on removing obstructions could begin without delay, and at the end of November the salvage teams had cleared a 25-foot deep channel as far as El Cap as well as opening Port Said harbour to vessels of up to 10,000 tons. The larger wrecks were cleared by two German heavy-lifting vessels, the *Energie* and *Ausdauer*, which were chartered by the British Admiralty from a Hamburg company.

In the middle of December the Anglo-French Salvage Command, under Rear-Admiral Jean Campion, consisted of forty vessels, nineteen of which were at work in the Canal Zone and the remainder standing by in case the word was given to begin clearance operations beyond El Cap. Proposals to this effect, however, were rejected outright by the Egyptian Government, which insisted that any further clearance must be undertaken by neutral salvage teams organised by the United Nations. But for this objection, the Anglo-French Salvage Command – which had already demonstrated the efficiency and speed with which it was capable of operating – could have cleared the whole of the Canal by the end of January 1957 at the latest. Instead, clearance work was to drag on for a further three months.

The United Nations finally undertook not only to clear the Canal, but also to raise the 40 million dollars or so that it would take to pay for the operation. The work was to be supervised by a 71-year-old American, General Raymond A. Wheeler, who as an engineer had been responsible for several major harbour clearance operations during World War II. After setting up his headquarters in Ismailia the general issued a timetable for the operation, which turned out in practice to be greatly over-optimistic. As a first step, he envisaged the extension as far as Suez – to be completed by early March – of the channel already cleared up to El Cap by the Anglo-French Salvage Command, allowing passage of vessels up to 10,000 tons. This task would mean the removal of nine wrecks, none of which could be salvaged; they would have to be dragged or floated clear of the projected shipping channel and dismembered at a later date. Some of the sunken vessels – those filled with concrete, for example – would have to be cut up under water, as would the El Ferdan railway bridge.

Once the 25-foot channel had been pushed through to Suez, work could begin on dismantling the wrecks and dredging the whole of the Canal, so that sea traffic of pre-October 1956 proportions could start to flow through it once more. Provision would also have to be made for a new fleet of tugs and maintenance vessels, for most of the original ones had been sunk by the Egyptians. At the same time, the UN salvage teams would set about restoring the harbour facilities at Port Said and Suez.

The assembly of Wheeler's salvage fleet took much longer than had been anticipated, and indeed it would probably not have been possible at all had not the Egyptian Government finally agreed, under strong pressure from the United Nations, that eighteen British and one French salvage vessels be retained to assist in clearing Port Said. The Egyptians, however, insisted on a number of conditions, among them that the crews of the British and French ships wore civilian clothes and did not venture ashore, that the vessels flew United Nations flags and that UN troops patrolled the banks of the Canal where they were operating.

At the end of December, therefore, General Wheeler's fleet comprised nineteen vessels, including the two German heavy lifting craft whose charter had been taken over by the United Nations. Their crews were a mixed bag, coming in the main from Belgium, Italy, the Netherlands, Denmark and Germany. On 24 January the British and French salvage ships departed, having completed their task of clearing Port Said; together they had cleared a total of 17,000 tons of wrecks, despite the difficult conditions and the unco-operative atmosphere in which they had been forced to work.

By 1 February the United Nations salvage fleet had succeeded in clearing about half the wrecks congesting the Canal between El Cap and Suez. Further operations were held up for some time by the LST *Akka*, which was crammed with concrete and firmly embedded in the side of the Canal, with much of her submerged under 40 feet of water. The German crews of the *Energie* and *Ausdauer* finally managed to work steel cables under her and hoist her on to an even keel, but it was two and a half weeks before her bulk was finally raised and removed.

The Canal clearance operation was completed on 7 May. The first British and French ships had already passed through the waterway in April, a few days before Nasser submitted a proposal to the United Nations promising the 'unimpeded use of the Canal by ships of all nations'. The United Nations accepted the proposal with some reservation, as there were still many loopholes in it; reservation or not it represented a political victory for the Egyptian Government, and the final seal was set upon it when, in July 1958, the Suez Canal Company recognised Egyptian ownership of the Canal.

The 'unimpeded use of the Canal by ships of all nations' was an invitation that did not extend to Israel, although the latter's victory in Sinai and the capture of the Straits of Tiran had given her access to the Red Sea and the Indian Ocean. Even so, Israel's freedom of navigation through the Straits of Tiran was bought at a heavy price: the withdrawal of her forces from Sinai and their replacement by a United Nations Expeditionary Force.

The inability of such a force to impose any kind of guarantee was to be clearly demonstrated ten years later, when it packed its bags and departed in the face of a massive Egyptian military build-up in Sinai. On 5 June 1967 Israel, to ensure her survival, once again attacked; this time her troops advanced to the edge of the Suez Canal, and the might of the Egyptian armed forces, painstakingly built-up over a decade, was shattered.

CHAPTER FIFTEEN

RETROSPECT

In the forty years since *Musketeer*, British forces have been involved in several 'police actions', notably the Kuwait crisis of 1961, the confrontation with Indonesia in Borneo, and operations against dissident tribesmen in the Radfan. They have also taken part in two large-scale conflicts, the Falklands War of 1982 and the Gulf War of 1991.

In terms of human life and material, the Falklands War was a costly venture. Much of the loss was suffered when the ships of the Task Force came under sustained and determined attack by enemy aircraft; apart from the Sea Harrier CAP and the various Fleet defence systems, there was nothing to stop them. What a different story it might have been had the Royal Navy retained at least one large carrier capable of operating long-range strike aircraft like the Buccaneer – aircraft which, setting aside all political objections, would have been in a position to mount devastating air attacks on airfields on the Argentinian mainland.

At Suez and in the Gulf, on the other hand, the enemy air forces were effectively neutralised before any action unfolded on the ground, and in both cases the mission was accomplished mainly by tactical strike aircraft. At Suez, the early airfield attacks by Main Force aircraft of RAF Bomber Command were conspicuous only by their failure, although others might term it a 'partial success'. The fact remains that in eighteen raids on thirteen targets, the Valiants and Canberras dropped 1,962 bombs, mostly 1,000-pounders, and of these – according to subsequent calculations by the Bomber Command Operational Research staff - 70 per cent fell in the target area but only 50 per cent fell within 650 yards of the aiming point. The post-strike reconnaissance photographs reproduced in this book speak for themselves.

Had the Egyptian Air Force chosen to oppose *Musketeer* before the arrival of the Naval Task Force, it was therefore in a position to do so, because most of the runways on its operational airfields were still intact. Had the Egyptians exercised the right option, they would have launched every available Ilyushin-28 jet bomber, escorted by MiG-15s, in a major assault on the Cyprus base, with the object of destroying as many Allied aircraft – especially Venoms and F-84s – as possible. Some would have fallen to the Cyprus air defences, but a great many would unquestionably have got through, and they would have inflicted horrendous damage on the crowded airfields, not to mention spreading panic among the Cypriot population. If that had happened, *Musketeer* might well have foundered before it even set sail.

But it did not happen, and the initial Allied reaction, apart from astonishment and relief, was to think that the the total lack of opposition reflected a breakdown in Egyptian morale resulting from the initial bombing attacks on the opening day of *Musketeer*. Subsequent reports, however, suggested that the Egyptians never attacked because they lacked a sufficient number of trained pilots, and Nasser was anxious to protect his largely inexperienced aircrew and their new Russian aircraft. The fact that most of the Il-28 force was immediately flown south to Luxor substantiates this theory. The aircraft that stayed on the northern airfields remained grounded, and in due course were sought out and destroyed by the Allied fighter-bombers.

The possibility that active resistance might have been put up by Russian and Czech pilots was considered by the Allied commanders, but the risk was considered acceptable. In fact, the risk of direct Russian involvement was never very great; the Russians were far too preoccupied with the Hungarian Uprising, a threat that was right on their doorstep and presented a major challenge to the communist domination of eastern Europe.

As to the failure of the initial airfield attacks, this was attributable to the fact that the Valiant squadrons were not fully worked up with their navigation and bombing systems, and the Canberra crews had to depend on visual bomb aiming, as their normal GH ground navigational aids were not available in the Middle East. Another problem with the Valiant was a tendency for part of the HE bomb load to 'hang up', and at high speed the bombs tended to stay with the aircraft immediately after release, suspended in the airflow. The problem was eventually cured by the fitting of baffles.

The ground-attack aircraft, both RAF and Navy, performed extremely well, the RAF's Venoms claiming the destruction of seventy-five MiG-15s with sixty more aircraft damaged. The Fleet Air Arm's Seahawks, Sea Venoms and Wyverns were very effective in the close support role; some of the pilots had seen combat in Korea three or four years earlier, flying piston-engined Sea Furies and Fireflies, and the lessons had been well learned. Another lesson learned by the Navy as a result of *Musketeer* was the value of the assault helicopter, and not long afterwards the carriers *Theseus* and *Ocean* were converted as helicopter assault ships. Later, the larger carriers *Bulwark* and *Albion* were completely refitted as commando carriers; they were subsequently to prove their worth in Kuwait, Malaysia and the troubled Persian Gulf states.

One immediate effect of *Musketeer* was that it brought a halt to the almost indecent speed with which Britain's conventional forces had been run down after the end of World War II. It was followed by a thorough streamlining of the armed services, with emphasis on the fast movement of air and surface forces to any part of the world at short notice. One of the early results was the re-equipment of the RAF's strategic transport squadrons, and an awareness of the fact that the type of aircraft used by them needed to keep pace with the times.

As a military operation, ignoring the muddled political direction that caused it to pass into history as a fiasco, *Musketeer* was a success as far as it went. Co-operation between the British and French was excellent throughout, and in many ways the French organisation was better than the British. In the final analysis it was remarkable that the operation unrolled so smoothly, given the fact that its planning had been ponderous and that it had been launched too late, and also that the plan itself had been subjected to last-minute changes. General Beaufre summed up the position clearly[17]:

> The first error was to change the plan less than a fortnight
> before the first launching date and substitute Port Said for the

Alexandria landing. Even if the Alexandria operation was less good, we would have done better to adhere to it at that late stage rather than involve ourselves in the vacillations of which we all know. At that time we ought to have insisted on launching the operation on 15 September, even if everything was not ready. The Egyptians were even less ready than we were and the Canal was still intact. Finally, by moving on Cairo, we should have made the object of the operation clear, which later it was not.

In the end, the whole business was reduced to a question of timing. A surprise attack on the Canal Zone, without the lengthy preliminary of air bombardment, might have prevented its blockage. Air drops from Cyprus on Port Said and Ismailia, supported by the hundred or so tanks for which landing craft were available and preceded by an air offensive lasting 24 hours or less, might have done the trick. Supporting vehicles could have been landed very quickly from half a dozen or so freighters, enabling the paratroops to hold on until the arrival of a reinforcement convoy. Their operations could have been supported by helicopters from the Royal Navy's carriers, which in any case would have been providing air cover from the outset, together with the strike aircraft from Cyprus.

The Canal might still have been captured intact had the Allied shipping not been subjected to so many loading delays after the decision to launch *Musketeer* was taken on 18 October. If the convoys had been ready to sail on that date, or even shortly afterwards, the first landings could have taken place on 1 November instead of five days later, by which time the Anglo-French operation had become inextricably linked in the eyes of the world with the Israeli offensive in Sinai. Apart from that, by 5 November the Israeli offensive had resulted in large numbers of Egyptian troops being withdrawn across the Canal; had they still been on the other side they could have been taken neatly in the rear by an Allied thrust along the waterway.

What would have happened if the Allies had ignored the ceasefire and progressed to the end of the Canal? What would have happened if they had attacked first, before Israel launched her offensive? What would have happened if Operation *Musketeer* had not taken place at all? These are questions that can never be answered. What does emerge from the unhappy affair, however, is a clear pointer to the development of conventional tactics and strategy within the military structures of France and Britain over the two decades that followed. To put it bluntly, *Musketeer* was worthwhile if only because it helped to sort out the muddled military thinking that had characterised the post-War years in both countries. Even in the nuclear age, armed forces must be geared towards fighting a conventional war. This was the lesson hammered home by *Musketeer*, even if the conflicts in Korea and Indo-China had not already done so. Unfortunately, the Americans – with all their hardware – were still learning it ten years later, in Vietnam.

Musketeer also pointed to the value of retaining an independent nuclear deterrent. At the climax of the operation, when the Russians were making thinly veiled threats of atomic retaliation against London and Paris, Britain's nuclear weapons were still in the testing stage, apart from a small stockpile of the first British atomic bomb (the MC. Mk 1 Blue Danube), and France had yet to test her first nuclear device. Even a nuclear force only fractionally as large as that of the Soviet Union still represented a powerful insurance against nuclear blackmail. As a result of *Musketeer*, the French accelerated their atomic weapons programme, which culminated in their first nuclear test in 1960, and before the end of 1956 they had issued a requirement for a nuclear delivery system, which resulted in the Dassault Mirage IV strategic bomber.

While the French decided to go their own way in the aftermath of Suez, the US and UK began to make concerted efforts to improve all aspects of their relationship. Three important meetings during 1957 laid the groundwork for the full resumption of co-operation in the nuclear weapons field. The first meeting, between British Defence Minister Duncan Sandys and Charles Wilson, US Secretary of Defense, was held between 28 January and 1 February in Washington. Several important subjects were discussed, including the adaptation of British bombers to carry US nuclear weapons, the storage of US nuclear bombs on British territory and the co-ordination of bombing targets between the Strategic Air Command and Bomber Command.

The second meeting, between Eisenhower and Harold Macmillan (who had replaced the ailing Anthony Eden as Prime

Minister in January 1957) took place from 21-24 February in Bermuda. From this meeting came the public announcement that American Thor ICBMs would be deployed to the UK. There were also two other matters covered in a secret annex, one regarding prior consultation on testing initiatives and the other concerning a common policy towards French nuclear ambitions. Another meeting between the two leaders, in Washington from 23-25 October, led to a 'Declaration of Common Purpose', which was to be a turning point in the sharing of information on nuclear matters. If *Musketeer* had caused a rift in Anglo-US relations, it was therefore quickly healed on the military front.

The most serious consequence of *Musketeer* for both Britain and France was the terrific blow the outcome of the operation dealt to both military and civilian morale. Even before the occupation ended, the morale of the troops was, quite understandably in the circumstances, visibly affected. This was particularly true of the French, who had already suffered the trauma of their defeat in Indo-China only two years earlier and who were now embroiled in the bitter conflict of Algeria. General Beaufre, in fact, was of the later opinion that the experience of Suez was in no small part to blame for the subsequent attitude of the French Army in Algeria, culminating in the revolt there of the 3rd Parachute Regiment in 1961 when the country was moving towards independence.

The adverse effect on morale would doubtless have been even greater if the operation had produced higher Allied casualty figures; as it was they were remarkably light. British casualties totalled 22 killed and 97 wounded (some by 'friendly fire'), while the French lost 10 killed and 33 wounded. Aircraft losses were 10, including the PR Canberra shot down over Syria; three of these aircraft were lost as the result of accidents. Egyptian military casualties are hard to ascertain, because many troops discarded their uniforms and fought in civilian clothes; the best estimates put Egyptian casualties in Port Said at 650 killed and 2,100 wounded, 900 seriously, with a further 100 killed and 250 wounded in Port Fuad. Taking the Sinai campaign into account, the total number of Egyptian dead was estimated at about 3,000.

Even before the last Allied troops had withdrawn from Egypt, Nasser was already using his powers of political rhetoric to turn his defeat into victory in the eyes of the Muslim world – a world in which the former great powers of Britain and France had been seriously discredited. They had lost credibility, too, in the eyes of other nations who viewed Nasser's regime as a threat – not in the main because they had launched the venture, but because they had hesitated and wavered for so long before launching it. The Allies could have attained their objectives if they had acted with the audacity and speed that had always characterised their previous military operations; that this did not happen was the fault mainly of the British Government, anxious to preserve its treaties with Jordan and to prevent its relations with the rest of the Arab countries from deteriorating still further.

In France, one man saw the possible future implications of *Musketeer* from a military standpoint perhaps more clearly than any other. In his temporary retirement at Colombey-les-deux-Eglises, General Charles de Gaulle was kept fully informed of events as they developed by an officer of the French General Staff, acting on the Government's authority. De Gaulle in no way disapproved of the Allies' initiative, though predictably he came out strongly against the leadership of the operation being vested in the British. He did, however, recognise that the Suez adventure had produced damaging undercurrents within the structure of the North Atlantic Treaty Organisation, of which both France and Britain were member nations. Within the NATO alliance, attitudes were sharply divided; some countries saw the Suez operation as simply a temporary quarrel in the strong Anglo-French-American relationship, others as a germ of dissent which, if it was allowed to grow, could lead to serious disruption of the plans for joint military action that had been so painstakingly laid by NATO over the preceding seven years.

At this point de Gaulle's doctrine *vis-a-vis* the Atlantic Alliance was already firmly established, but the Suez affair was to provide him with a justification, or at least a pretext, for his later actions leading up to the French withdrawal from NATO. Announcing the French Government's decision to pull out of NATO at the beginning of 1966, de Gaulle stated that[18]

> In 1956, at the time of the Suez affair, neither France nor Britain had been attacked by Egypt. When Marshal Bulganin,

in the name of the Soviet Union, threatened to send rockets on Paris and London, the United States showed evidence by their attitude that their obligations to NATO did not enter into the matter.

In fact, this was not strictly true; as we have seen, Strategic Air Command's alert state was quietly stepped up in response to the Soviet threat, while the US Navy ordered all major Fleet units to sea under conditions of maximum readiness. However, de Gaulle went on to apply what he considered to be a precedent to a hypothetical situation. If the danger of world war were to result from an attack on Communist China by the United States, and if the Soviet Union were dragged into the conflict in the process of escalation and launched an attack on the USA, France should show no more concern than did the United States at the time of Suez. He concluded: 'We wish to retain the right to refuse to become involved in any conflict, just as the Americans did at Suez.'[19]

The Suez Expedition, then, produced undertones and repercussions in both the military and political sense, which were still being felt many years later. It reinforced an already widely held belief that the days of imperialism were gone, and it imbued the French with an overwhelming desire to acquire a commanding position in Europe, both economically and militarily. Unfortunately, it took Britain much longer to realise that Europe was where her true destiny lay.

If there is to be a last word on the subject, perhaps it is fitting that it should go to Winston Churchill, Anthony Eden's father-in-law. On 20 November 1956, Jock Colville, Churchill's Private Secretary, dined with the great man. The eventual withdrawal of the Anglo-French forces had been accepted by Eden as the one condition on which President Eisenhower and the United States would continue to support Britain. Speaking of Eden's decision to attack Egypt, Colville asked Churchill[20]:

'If you had been Prime Minister, would you have done this?' Churchill's reply was simple:

'I would never have dared, and if I had dared, I would never have dared stop.'

REFERENCES

1   Page 22: General André Beaufre, *The Suez Expedition* (Faber, 1969).
2   23. Proceedings No 3, Royal Air Force Historical Society *A Seminar on the Suez Operation*, 1988.
3   29. David Young, *Four-Five – the Story of 45 Commando Royal Marines, 1943–71* (Leo Cooper, 1972).
4   38. Quoted in Keith Kyle: *Suez* (Weidenfeld, 1989).
5   46. Proceedings No 3, Royal Air Force Historical Society *A Seminar on the Suez Operation*, 1988.
6   56. Ibid.
7   58. Ibid.
8   62. Young, *Four-Five*.
9   64. Proceedings No 3, RAF Hist Soc.
10 68. Ibid.
11 69. Ibid.
12 76. Ibid.
13 80. Ibid.
14 98. Royal Air Force Flying Review, Vol 12 No 5, January 1957.
15 116. Beaufre, *The Suez Expedition*.
16 120. Quoted in Keith Kyle, *Suez*.
17 129. Beaufre, *The Suez Expedition*.
18 133. Ibid.
19 134. (1). Ibid.
20 134. (2). Martin Gilbert, *Churchill* (Heinemann 1991).

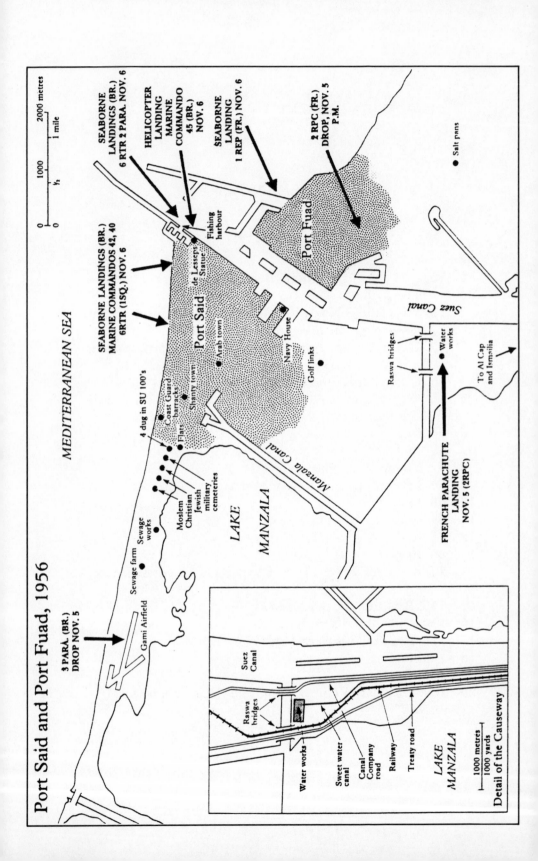

Port Said and Port Fuad, 1956

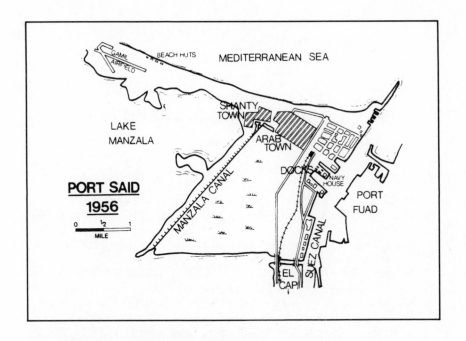

MEDITERRANEAN SEA

GAMIL AIRFIELD BEACH HUTS

SHANTY TOWN

LAKE MANZALA

ARAB TOWN

DOCKS

NAVY HOUSE

PORT SAID
1956

0   ½   1
MILE

MANZALA CANAL

PORT FUAD

SUEZ CANAL

EL CAP

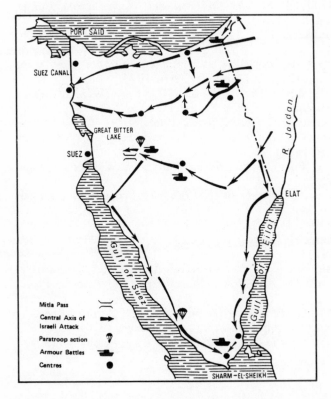

PORT SAID

SUEZ CANAL

GREAT BITTER LAKE

SUEZ

R Jordan

ELAT

Gulf of Suez

Gulf of Elat

Mitla Pass	)(
Central Axis of Israeli Attack	→
Paratroop action	☥
Armour Battles	▬
Centres	●

SHARM – EL – SHEIKH

SELECT BIBLIOGRAPHY

Barker, A. J.: *Suez: the Seven-Day War* (Faber & Faber, 1964).

Beaufre, General André: *The Suez Expedition 1956* (Faber & Faber, 1969).

Black, Ian, and Morris, Benny: *Israel's Secret Wars* (Hamish Hamilton, 1991).

Braddon, Russell: *Suez, Splitting of a Nation* (Collins, 1973).

Carlton, David: *Anthony Eden. A Biography* (Allen Lane, 1981).

Carlton, David: *Britain and the Suez Crisis* (ICBH/Blackwell, 1988).

Cavenagh, Sandy: *Airborne to Suez* (William Kimber, 1965).

Childers, Erskine B: *The Road to Suez* (MacGibbon and Kee, 1962).

Churchill, Randolph S: *The Rise and Fall of Sir Anthony Eden* (MacGibbon and Kee, 1962).

Crankshaw, Edward (Ed): *Khrushchev Remembers* (Andre Deutsch, 1971).

Crosbie, Sylvia K: *A Tacit Alliance: France and Israel from Suez to the Six-Day War* (Princeton University Press, 1974).

Dayan, General Moshe: *Diary of the Sinai Campaign* (Weidenfeld and Nicolson, 1976).

Eden, Sir Anthony: *Full Circle* (Cassell, 1960).

Fawzi, Mahmoud: *Suez 1956. An Egyptian Perspective* (Shorouk International, 1987).

Ferrell, Robert (Ed): *The Eisenhower Diaries* (W.W. Norton, New York, 1981).

Fullick, Roy, and Power, Geoffrey: *Suez: the Double War* (Hamish Hamilton, 1979).

Gaujac, Paul: *Suez 1956* (Lavauzelle, Paris, 1987).

Heikal, Mohamed: *Nasser: The Cairo Documents* (New English Library, 1972).

Heikal, Mohamed: *Cutting the Lion's Tail* (Andre Deutsch, 1986).

Herzog, Chaim: *The Arab–Israeli Wars* (Arms and Armour Press, 1982).

Jackson, Robert: *Canberra – the Operational Record* (Airlife, 1988).

Jackson, Robert: *The Israeli Air Force Story* (Stacey, 1970).

Jackson, Robert: *Suez 1956: Operation Musketeer* (Ian Allan, 1980).

Jackson, Robert: *V-Bombers* (Ian Allan, 1981).

Kyle, Keith: *Suez* (Weidenfeld and Nicolson, 1989).

Lee, Air Chief Marshal Sir David: *Wings in the Sun: a History of the Royal Air Force in the Mediterranean 1945–1986.* (HMSO 1989).

Love, Kennett: *Suez: the Twice-Fought War* (Longman, 1970).

Luttwak, Edward, and Horowitz, Dan: *The Israeli Army* (Allen Lane, 1975).

Macksey, Kenneth: *The Tanks. The History of the Royal Tank Regiment* (Arms and Armour Press, 1979).

Mansfield, Peter: *The British in Egypt* (Weidenfeld and Nicolson 1974).

O'Ballance, Edgar: *The Sinai Campaign* (Faber & Faber, 1989).

Pineau, Christian: *1956 Suez* (Robert Laffont, Paris, 1976).

RAF Historical Society: Proceedings No 3, *A Seminar on the Air Aspects of the Suez Campaign, 1956* (London, 1988).

Robertson, Terence: *Crisis. The Inside Story of the Suez Conspiracy* (Hutchinson, 1965).

Shuckburgh, Sir Evelyn: *Descent to Suez* (Weidenfeld and Nicolson, 1986).

Thomas, Hugh: *The Suez Affair* (Weidenfeld and Nicolson, 1967).

Young, David: *Four Five – the Story of 45 Commando Royal Marines, 1943–71* (Leo Cooper, 1972).

INDEX

141

INDEX

143